# RUNNING ON AIR

# RUNNING
# ON

From BBC Headlines to
Life-Changing Fitness

SC
RA

# RUNNING ON AIR

## From BBC Headlines to Life-Changing Finish Lines

## SOPHIE RAWORTH

BLOOMSBURY SPORT
LONDON · OXFORD · NEW YORK · NEW DELHI · SYDNEY

BLOOMSBURY SPORT
Bloomsbury Publishing Plc
50 Bedford Square, London, WC1B 3DP, UK
Bloomsbury Publishing Ireland Limited
29 Earlsfort Terrace, Dublin 2, D02 AY28, Ireland

BLOOMSBURY, BLOOMSBURY SPORT and the Diana logo are trademarks of
Bloomsbury Publishing Plc

First published in Great Britain 2026

Copyright © Sophie Raworth, 2026

Sophie Raworth has asserted her right under the Copyright, Designs and Patents Act, 1988,
to be identified as Author of this work

For legal purposes the Acknowledgements on p. 245
constitute an extension of this copyright page

All rights reserved. No part of this publication may be: i) reproduced or transmitted in any form, electronic or mechanical, including photocopying, recording or by means of any information storage or retrieval system without prior permission in writing from the publishers; or ii) used or reproduced in any way for the training, development or operation of artificial intelligence (AI) technologies, including generative AI technologies. The rights holders expressly reserve this publication from the text and data mining exception as per Article 4(3) of the Digital Single Market Directive (EU) 2019/790

Bloomsbury Publishing Plc does not have any control over, or responsibility for, any third-party websites referred to or in this book. All internet addresses given in this book were correct at the time of going to press. The author and publisher regret any inconvenience caused if addresses have changed or sites have ceased to exist, but can accept no responsibility for any such changes

The information contained in this book is provided by way of general guidance in relation to the specific subject matters addressed herein, but it is not a substitute for specialist advice. It should not be relied on for medical, health-care, pharmaceutical or other professional advice on specific dietary or health needs. This book is sold with the understanding that the author and publisher are not engaged in rendering medical, health or any other kind of personal or professional services. The reader should consult a competent medical or health professional before adopting any of the suggestions in this book or drawing inferences from it. The author and publisher specifically disclaim, as far as the law allows, any responsibility from any liability, loss or risk (personal or otherwise) which is incurred as a consequence, directly or indirectly, of the use and applications of any of the contents of this book.

A catalogue record for this book is available from the British Library

Library of Congress Cataloguing-in-Publication data has been applied for

ISBN: HB: 978-1-3994-2633-6; eBook: 978-1-3994-2637-4

2 4 6 8 10 9 7 5 3 1

Typeset in Lumina Datamatics Ltd
Printed and bound in Great Britain by Clays Ltd, Elcograf S.p.A.

To find out more about our authors and books visit www.bloomsbury.com
and sign up for our newsletters
For product safety related questions contact productsafety@bloomsbury.com

For Ella, Georgie and Ollie.
You never regret a run...

# Contents

| | | |
|---|---|---|
| 1 | Hitting the ground, running | 1 |
| 2 | Playing the long game | 17 |
| 3 | Mission to the Stars | 43 |
| 4 | Preparing to go the extra mile | 69 |
| 5 | Feeling the fear and doing it anyway | 89 |
| 6 | Going all in on the Highway to Hell | 99 |
| 7 | Galloping to a place on the podium | 123 |
| 8 | What about your knees? | 131 |
| 9 | Peak Time | 143 |
| 10 | Harnessing the mind | 161 |
| 11 | More than just a run in the park | 185 |
| 12 | Stopped in my tracks | 197 |
| 13 | The circle of life | 217 |
| | *Acknowledgements* | 245 |

# I

## *Hitting the ground, running*

It is the roaring crowd that wakes me. Shouting, cheering, the sound of people all around me. I listen, confused, eyes closed. A woman's voice. 'Do you know where you are? Sophie?' I have no idea at all. A pop concert in Roundhay Park in Leeds? That's what springs to mind, not that I have ever been to one there before. I am lying on my back. I am wet. Why am I wet? Someone is pulling at my clothes, prodding me, tugging at my shorts. That's what makes me open my eyes, fast. I have an oxygen mask on. People in green are leaning right over me, peering at me, speaking to me. I can't make sense of them. I raise my head with difficulty. And then I see them, a streaming mass of people running, staggering, limping after each other. Hundreds of them, on the Embankment by the Thames, all heading in the same direction, Big Ben in sight. This is the London Marathon. I should be running with them towards Buckingham Palace. Instead, I seem to have collapsed.

The lady peering over me is called Trish. That's what she tells me as she pushes ice under my running vest and down my shorts. I shiver. The mask over my face makes me panic. I feel claustrophobic. I can't breathe. 'Am I going to die?' I ask her over and over again. I have been unconscious for about 20 minutes, Trish tells me. My temperature is 41.2°C. I scan her face for signs of alarm. They're taking my temperature 'internally'. It is not somewhere I have ever had a thermometer before. Exposed, on a stretcher on the kerbside, crowds all around me, glancing down, cameras, phones in hand. 'Can you move me?' I gasp through the hissing plastic mask. 'I'm on the telly.' This is not a sight I want to see splashed across the *Daily Mail*.

I'm wheeled further away from the roadside into Temple Place, where a St John Ambulance first-aid station has been set up. It is quieter here. I lie surrounded by a few other beached runners on stretchers and try to stop the waves of panic that are seizing my chest. I feel like I'm going to suffocate. 'I need more oxygen! Can you turn it up?' I keep mumbling at Trish. She tells me to breathe in deeply, that I will be all right. I lie there listening to the cheers and clapping and happiness, to the mass of people who have surged on to the streets to help propel exhausted runners along the last 2 miles of this race. I stare at the blue sky and the big, billowy, thick clouds, dramatic shapes, lumpy towering heights. I'm not religious. But those clouds make me think of leaving here. Of going to heaven. This can't be the end, can it? I lie there watching the dashing whiteness and think how utterly ridiculous this is. How totally stupid. Here I am, at the age of 42, running my first marathon to raise money for three women who have all died from cancer far too soon, leaving young children behind. Now, I am going to die as well while my three children, all under the age of seven, are waiting for me with my husband and parents in the grandstand at the finish line. What an idiot I am.

# HITTING THE GROUND, RUNNING

I have never blacked out before. Nor have I ever had people fussing over me with what looks like a shade of fear in their eyes. My mind is foggy. It takes me a while to make sense of the sequence of events that have landed me here. Trish unpins my race number from my Cancer Research running vest. 'SOPHIE' is emblazoned across the front. On the back I've written my name and address and an emergency contact number that I never imagined I would need. Trish uses it to call my husband. No answer. She leaves a message. 'We have your wife here at St John Ambulance. She is OK. We are looking after her. Do call us back on this number.' He doesn't. She tries again. And then I hear my own voice talking back at her. It's my voicemail, not his. I realise that in a rush of pre-race nerves I wrote my own number on the back of my race bib. I have been lying here for almost an hour now. My family will be wondering, worrying about where I am. I try to remember Richard's phone number so Trish can call him. Nothing. My memory isn't working. My dad's number, after decades of dialling it, has vanished too. I gaze up at the sky again, trying to reboot my mind. But it won't work. The only number that I can recall is the one for my childhood home, where my parents still live, but my memory throws up its 1980s '01' London telephone code. No use now. And anyway, they're not at home. They're on The Mall scanning the exhausted runners, searching for me.

My temperature is coming down. Trish takes off the oxygen mask. I can breathe more easily now. Chinks of memory return. I'm supposed to be going on holiday tomorrow. *That won't happen*, I think. But at least it doesn't look like I am going to die. Hospital maybe. But not death. I wonder where Charlie is, my friend who I have trained with all winter and who stood with me on the start line however many hours ago. We were so nervous. She and I had spent the night in a hotel by Tower Bridge. I hardly slept, afraid of the distance ahead. I have never run 26.2 miles before. I took ibuprofen to mask the lingering aches from months of running on legs that had hardly been run on since my youth. I have trained hard for six months. I haven't cut corners. I had signed up with a coach, Karen Weir. I did what she said. I followed her training plan to the letter. It went well. I got faster. So much so that a few weeks before the marathon, she called me to say she was pretty sure I could run it in under 4 hours, the magic number most first-timers fantasise about breaking. I couldn't believe it. Nor, as it turned out, could my husband, who had always been the runner in our house. Richard had spent years trying to coax me out of the door with his enthusiasm for a short run around the local park. I had tried it a couple of times when we first met. I insisted on water (not needed on a 3-mile slow run) and I insisted on stopping. A lot. He didn't persist for long. With three marathons to his name, 4 hours 15 minutes was his fastest time. So, the notion of me beating him on my first marathon outing was too much. He looked at me wide-eyed. 'If you run the London Marathon in under 4 hours,' he declared defiantly, 'I will run round Berkeley Square naked!' The gauntlet was thrown down.

    Charlie and I had travelled from our hotel at Tower Bridge to the start line on Blackheath on board an old double-decker bus. It had been laid on by the marathon organisers and was packed with VIPs and 'celebrity runners'. We sat on the top deck like naughty kids fizzing with nervous energy, watching through misted-up windows as the streets of South East London fell away behind us. Then suddenly the road opened up and we were on the hill, on wide open parkland with blue skies and sweeping views of London in front of us. Huge hot air balloons, tethered to the ground, marked the various start points. Thousands of people moving slowly in the same direction, barely speaking, kitbags slung over their shoulders, extra layers to keep warm in the early morning chill. More than 35,000 people, mostly quiet, psyching themselves up for the 26.2 miles ahead. In stark contrast, cheery voices on loudspeakers echoed around the park, their crackling energy greeting us all as we scanned the signs to find our allotted start zone. And then the nervous wait began. Charlie and I sat down and drank water, fiddled about with our running kit, counted and re-counted the energy gels we had brought with us before zipping them back up in our running belts. We queued for the loo, sat down again, drank more water, queued for the loo again. There was nervous banter, photographers in a line waiting to get pictures of the famous faces in our cordoned-off area. The Olympians James Cracknell and Matthew Pinsent, the model Nell McAndrew, the singer Will Young. Running shoes were laced and relaced. Toes Vaselined against the pounding ahead. I glanced constantly at my running watch. The time sped up. Another queue for the loo, just in case, and then I swallowed two more ibuprofen to try to soften the pain ahead. We threw our kitbags on to big open-sided lorries that would meet us at the finish line in The Mall.

And then we headed to our start line. I stood right at the front, mixed in with the Olympians and lithe-looking runners, heart beating, adrenaline high. It's a curious feeling that wait at the start. Months of training throughout a cold winter, months of imagining this moment and suddenly you're here, stomach tingling, heart beating, springing up and down on your feet to keep warm, copying other runners who look like they know what they're doing as they stretch and bounce about. The klaxon sounded. We shuffled to the starting gantry, like a nervous herd of cattle. I hit start on my running watch, hugged Charlie and shot off. Far too fast. A golden rule of marathon running already broken.

The first few miles were mesmerising. The streets were lined with people cheering us all on, local residents standing in their front gardens, sipping tea, waving. I couldn't stop smiling. The London Marathon has so many runners that it needs several start lines to funnel the masses along separate routes to begin with. After a couple of miles, we all then merged into a streaming mass of sweating, heavy-breathing humanity with the rhythmic sound of thousands of pairs of feet beating down on the tarmac as we glimpsed the Thames for the first time. It was exhilarating. I kept glancing at my watch. Karen, my coach, had warned me to keep it steady at the start, to hold back and not set off too quickly. I was supposed to be running each mile in just under 9 minutes, which would get me to the end in under 4 hours. I was already going too fast. Water stations came and went. I grabbed bottles at a few, ran past others. I didn't want to be stopping in another queue for the loo. I had a time to beat, a bet to win.

# HITTING THE GROUND, RUNNING

I scanned the crowd for people I knew and saw none. I was overtaken by beer bottles, a star, superheroes, a wooden spoon. Then the screaming started. I couldn't look round to see what the commotion was, too worried about tripping. But the crowd was focused on something going on behind me. I had my earphones in, my running playlist on, but the music was being drowned out by the noise. A bend in the road and finally I was able to glance back. White flesh, wobbling tummy, leopard skin straps covering very little, nipples taped up, black wig, black moustache. A man in a leopard-skin mankini was right behind me. He was almost naked, and the crowd were loving him. I laughed out loud. But after a while the ripple of screams and catcalls coming our way became too much. After a winter of training mostly on my own or with small groups of friends, the constant noise and cheering became overwhelming. I pushed on to try to escape the din.

Another wall of noise hit us as we turned the corner on to Tower Bridge, one of the most iconic moments in this race as you approach the halfway point. Vast crowds stood 10 deep on either side with banners held aloft bearing the names of loved ones or slogans – 'Pain is temporary, glory is forever' – to spur us all on. I ran across that bridge trying to soak it all in, scanning the faces, catching people's eyes. 'It's that newsreader,' I kept hearing people say as they pointed at me. Others just shouted my name; some who knew me from television, others who were just reading it on my running vest. I'd never had my name yelled at me so much for so long. *This must be what it is like to be a teacher*, I thought, *with your name being called out over and over again.*

Was it on Tower Bridge that my first marathon started to go wrong? I do remember a rising sense of anxiety. I could see the hotel right by the bridge where Charlie and I had just spent the night. I had a sudden urge to stop. We were 12 miles in, not even halfway. My legs felt OK. But I was getting tired, and it was getting hot. Much hotter than I'd thought it would be. I was taking my energy gels every 5 miles, the sugar and electrolytes needed to fuel the body. 'No water needed' was written on the packaging. It was only much later that I realised it meant no water was needed to *digest* them, not no water at all.

As we came off the bridge we turned right towards the Docklands and Canary Wharf. On the other side of the road, heading back towards us, were the fastest club runners, who were already on the final stretch to Big Ben and The Mall with just 4 miles to go. I tried to distract myself for a while by scanning their faces, many of them etched with pain. I could see how much this was going to hurt later. We were heading the other way towards the toughest part of the race, where the crowds thin and your confidence falters. Marathon running is a mental battle, as well as a physical test. And my mind was starting to struggle. I never realised how lonely you could feel running with thousands of people. I was surrounded, yet I was with no one I knew, no one to talk to, no one to help me gauge the race I was in. I gave up on my headphones. I'd had to boost the volume so much to hear the music that it was becoming deafening. Too much noise in my head. But after months of training with music, losing it shook my already wobbly mind.

Between 18 and 21 miles is the hardest zone of a marathon. It is when the doubts can really kick in. The furthest

I had ever run was 20 miles in a race a few months before. As I tipped over that mark into the unknown zone, I was starting to feel strange. I began having a desperate craving for oranges. People had been handing out chopped-up fruit earlier in the race and I scanned the crowds for the orange slices that my body seemed to need. My legs were feeling heavy. It was hot but I was cold. I had goosebumps. My skin prickled. With 5 miles to go, I assumed this was normal for the last stretch of a marathon. So, I pushed on. I seemed to be on track for my sub-4-hour goal, though my mind was by now struggling to make sense of the timings. I saw a familiar face in the crowd, a friend of my husband's, and tried to wave but it was strangely hard to turn and look. I needed all my energy just to keep moving forwards. I was back near Tower Bridge by now, heading down towards the Embankment, the crowds thick again, another wall of noise. It was dizzying. My heart seemed to be beating fast. I was hot. I was cold. Light-headed. Was this the dreaded 'marathon wall' that every runner fears, when you are suddenly depleted of all energy in the final few miles and forced to walk? Had I hit it?

As I emerged from a tunnel on to the Embankment, Big Ben in sight at last, it wasn't a wall that I hit, but a crash barrier on the side of the road. I bounced off it, stumbled, hit it again. 'Come on Sophie! You can do it!' shouted a man on the other side of it. I looked down at my feet. My heart was racing now. My feet were weaving all over the road. *This must be the wall*, I thought. And then I hit the ground. I don't remember that bit. In fact, it wasn't until years later that I found out what had happened, when I met a man who'd been in the crowd and had seen me collapse. I was struggling to go in a straight line, he said, and then I just stopped, crumpled to the ground and lay there not moving. A policeman, who happened to be standing nearby, ran over to me and with help managed to carry me towards St John Ambulance staff and a stretcher. They then wheeled me to their pop-up aid station a little further along the road in Temple Place. And that's where Trish took over. 'We were really worried about you,' she later told me. I was unconscious for a good 20 minutes and my temperature was sky-high. It was hot that day, much warmer than forecast. The 2011 London Marathon turned out to be one of the hottest on record at 20°C. The medical team were pretty sure I had heatstroke, a medical emergency that can kill you if it's not dealt with fast enough. I hadn't drunk enough water. I had taken too many ibuprofen, which I only later discovered can cause serious problems with your kidneys if you're dehydrated. My body had lost its ability to cool itself down. In short, I was boiling over. My blood pressure was very low. I needed oxygen to breathe. Trish sponged me down with plenty of cold water and pushed more ice under my running vest. They needed to get my temperature down quickly. 'If it stays too high for too long, there is a serious chance of heart and kidney failure, stroke or even death,' a doctor later told me.

I wasn't the only one who got into serious trouble that day. Ninety runners ended up in hospital. Thousands more were treated by first-aiders along the route, many of them because of the heat. It was only weeks later that I discovered that I had shared my medical tent with the Kaiser Chiefs' frontman, Ricky Wilson. Like me, it was his first marathon, and like me, he went off too fast. Much too fast as it turned out. He was at the halfway point over Tower Bridge a whole 45 minutes earlier than he had planned to be, flying along with a 3-hour pacer, thinking how great that he could keep up. And then he too collapsed in the tunnel that leads on to the Embankment, just 2 miles from the end. He doesn't remember very much about it either. He ended up in an ambulance and then in a medical tent, completely confused. 'I didn't really know who I was or where I was,' he tells me years later. 'I just had a crushing sense of disappointment that I hadn't achieved something that I thought I could do.' They kept asking him questions – his name, his age, who the prime minister was. He couldn't remember. 'The prime ministers seem to be changing a lot,' he said, bluffing. He had been there quite some time when I was carried in and laid out unconscious on a bed on the other side of the tent. 'You're not the only famous person in here now, you know,' someone told him. 'It was really weird,' he says, 'and I'm really sorry to have to tell you this, but they suddenly said they were going to have to turn me over to face the wall because they needed to give you a suppository up your bottom. I think it was to stop you from dying! But they turned me back over too soon. I knew you really well from the TV. I grew up in Yorkshire and watched you on the local BBC news, on Look North. But that was not the way I imagined I would first meet Sophie Raworth. Let's just say I feel like I know you quite intimately now,' he says and then bursts out laughing.

Ricky Wilson is long gone by the time I am able to sit up. He has jumped in a black cab and is heading home with sore legs and a very bruised ego. He does finish the marathon but not until five days later when he goes back with friends to the exact place he collapsed and runs from there to the finish line in The Mall. 'I did it in a personal best of about 5 days, 19 hours and 14 seconds or something like that,' he jokes. And he has not run another marathon since.

Trish offers me a cup of tea, which I drink greedily with spoonfuls of sugar. My mind is clearing at last. I have been here for a good 90 minutes or so. My friend, Charlie, must have finished by now. She'll be wondering where I am. Phone numbers are jumbling through my head still. Like a roulette wheel, I suddenly land on one and ask Trish to dial it quickly before it disappears again. My dad is there, answering fast. I can hear the fear in his voice and the relief at hearing mine. 'Where are you, Soph?' he shouts from the finish line. I can hardly hear him. I tell him I'm OK, not to worry. I'm with St John Ambulance. 'I'll get to you as soon as I can,' I say. I've ticked off death and hospital from my list of possible outcomes. Maybe I'll get to go on holiday after all. 'So, what happens now?' I ask Trish, as the sugary tea kicks in. 'You're only 2 miles from The Mall. We'll put you on a bus to the finish line,' she says. I know I'm on the mend because I feel instantly indignant and laugh. I was running this race for Cancer Research. Friends, family and complete strangers have so far sponsored me £12,000. But the deal was that I had to run the whole marathon. I can't quit 2 miles from the end! 'Put me on a bus? No way!' I say to Trish, laughing. 'I can't go on a bus to the end after all these people have sponsored me! I have to finish it! I will walk to the end!' Doctors are consulted. There are some quizzical looks exchanged. The medics are clearly not convinced by this idea. We strike a deal. If I can walk in a straight line, they will let me go back out on to the Embankment and rejoin my fellow runners. But no more running, they say sternly. I must walk to the end.

Another cup of tea and plenty more sugar and I'm back on my feet. A couple of medics watch me closely as I follow the cracks in the pavement, back and forth, for a few minutes, feet no longer weaving, a straight line maintained. Finally, a little bemused, they agree to let me go. I give Trish a huge hug and thank her for looking after me. And then I am back into the masses, though they've definitely slowed down since I was last among them. Almost 6 hours after I started, I can see Big Ben again. I am on my way home. I walk away from the St John Ambulance station. 'Come on, Sophie, you can do it,' people start shouting. I feel cross. 'I should have finished this hours ago,' I want to shout back. Instead, I smile and walk on. As soon as the St John Ambulance bay is out of sight, I break into a forbidden jog. I need this to be over now. Big Ben, Parliament Square, Birdcage Walk, Buckingham Palace... I have run down here so many times on training runs recently and imagined, with tears in my eyes, what this moment would be like. I would arrive triumphant, in under 4 hours, crowds cheering, family waving, TV cameras rolling, a medal around my neck.

Instead, as I turn the corner past Buckingham Palace, the grandstand is being dismantled, barriers are being packed away, the crowds have thinned, Sue Barker and the BBC cameras are long gone. And so, 6 hours, 22 minutes and 57 seconds after I set off from Blackheath, I finally cross the finish line, dry-eyed. My three-year-old son is fast asleep in his pushchair. My five- and six-year-old daughters come running over. My parents and husband look utterly relieved to see me at last. Do I detect a glimmer of relief of a different kind on my husband's face as well? He has won the bet. No naked run in Mayfair after all. I just feel cross. Cross and exhausted. A little embarrassed too. This is not how it was supposed to have ended. This was not the marathon story I wanted to tell. There's one BBC camera crew still milling about. They grab me and put me live on to the BBC News Channel. Behind me the barriers are being piled up and volunteers are picking up the last of the rubbish on The Mall. I explain what has just happened. 'I've had a nightmare,' I say. 'I was out cold, I collapsed!' The presenter sounds almost embarrassed for me and keeps moving me on with questions about my motivation for running and the atmosphere on the streets. *I collapsed! I blacked out! That's the story!* I keep thinking, as my journalistic instinct kicks in. *You should be asking me about that!* But he doesn't.

Afterwards I head home, a little deflated and increasingly sore. I don't know what I did when I blacked out or how I fell, but my knee is really hurting now.

The next day I am on the front page of the *Daily Telegraph*. A big photo of me at the finish line clutching my medal around my neck, grinning madly. I look like I'm about to strangle myself with it. The headline reads: 'Plucky Sophie collapses in London Marathon but carries on'. I feel ashamed. And then the messages start coming from friends congratulating me on getting to the end. People on Twitter seem amazed that I had got up and finished. Piers Morgan, who has already sponsored me a lot of money, emails to say he is now doubling his contribution; 'danger money' he calls it. And many more follow him. Thousands more pounds roll in to my sponsorship page. In the end I raise more than £24,000 for Cancer Research. My mum rings me to check I am recovering. 'Oh Sophie! I was so worried about you,' she says. 'I thought something really terrible had happened. We heard nothing from you for more than 5 hours! You won't run another marathon, will you? Please don't?' And I know as she says it that that is exactly what I will do.

## 2

## *Playing the long game*

2006 was the year I lost my job and started running. Proper running. Long-distance running with a training plan and my first race in sight. It is only now, more than 20 years later, that I realise just how intricately the two events were connected. How being moved suddenly off the BBC's *Six O'Clock News* would push me into something that would change my life and fill me with a new strength and inner confidence that had eluded me for years.

I was 38 and had just given birth to my second child, Georgia. She was eight weeks old. In February my husband and I flew to the Canary Islands with our new baby and her 18-month-old sister, Ella, in search of sunshine, warmth and sleep. We had only been there for a couple of days when I got a message from work. The head of news wanted to discuss something with me. I hadn't had much contact with the BBC since I had disappeared off on maternity leave in the autumn. My world had been overtaken by babies, nappies and exhaustion. The message from work was unexpected. I knew something was up.

While the children were having their afternoon nap, I climbed up on to the roof terrace of the house we were staying in, out into a bright white haze of heat. I called my boss. I sat totally still listening as he told me that the veteran newsreader, Anna Ford, was leaving the *One O'Clock News* in April. He wanted me to take on her job. It was a great opportunity, he said. My own bulletin, good hours, something I would do well. The only problem was I didn't want to do it. I had only been on the *Six O'Clock News* for a couple of years, co-presenting it with George Alagiah, and I wanted to go back there. 'What if I don't want to move? What if I want to stay on the *Six* with George?' I asked him nervously, a sudden shiver in the sunshine. 'We really want you to do the *One O'Clock News*. That's what we have decided,' he said. I felt sick. I was on maternity leave. Could they move me? I didn't know. My brain was foggy. I was already feeling out of control with my old life of child-free whims disappearing fast behind me. And now the job that I had felt so proud to be doing was vanishing too. My boss didn't need to tell me who would be replacing me. The *Breakfast TV* presenter and recently crowned winner of *Strictly Come Dancing*, Natasha Kaplinsky, had stepped into the role while I was on maternity leave.

I sat stunned in the Spanish sunshine. Then I called Jay Hunt, the woman who had been in charge of the *Six O'Clock News* when I first joined the programme. A fiercely intelligent editor, who'd become a good friend, she had recently moved on to a bigger role on BBC One. She listened as I spilled out what had just happened. 'Just play the long game, Sophie,' she said calmly. It is still to this day one of the best pieces of advice anyone has ever given me. 'Do what they want you to do. Make the lunchtime news work for you. The *One O'Clock News* is still a great job with the same salary. You've got small kids; the hours will be good. You can get home for bathtime. Don't kick up a fuss now. They've clearly made their minds up about Natasha doing the *Six*. The thing about jobs on TV is that sometimes your face just won't fit and there'll be absolutely nothing you can do about it. So go back to work, smile, keep your head down, do a good job. Focus on the long game.'

I did what she said. I agreed to take on the *One O'Clock News*. I smiled outwardly as I told my colleagues and friends just how good the new job would be now that I had two children under the age of two. Inside, I felt crushed. George Alagiah and I had launched the BBC's new-look *Six O'Clock News* just three years earlier in 2003. It was a double-headed bulletin with the two of us presenting together every night. George was the charming experienced foreign correspondent who'd been brought into the studio. I was fresh off a five-year stint on *Breakfast News* with Jeremy Bowen and still in my early 30s. I had been amazed and so proud when I was asked to be the new presenter on the *Six*. Now I was being moved and there was nothing I could do about it.

Days later an email arrived out of the blue. The Olympian Brendan Foster was inviting me to be a 'celebrity runner' in the Great North Run in September, a half marathon from Newcastle to South Shields on the coast, crossing the famous Tyne Bridge. It's 13.1 miles of road running in a race that has now become the biggest half marathon in the world, with more than 60,000 people taking part. I had never run more than a couple of miles in my life and that was years ago. 'Don't think, just say yes, sign up, I'll run it with you,' said my husband, Richard, who knew I needed something to distract me from what had just happened.

I bought a pair of trainers. I was on maternity leave for four more months. I was now going back to a different job. Work could wait. I accepted the challenge. Richard was delighted. I would have to do the training. I would have to lose the weight I had gained during pregnancy. I would have to get fit. No one else could do it for me. This was something I was going to have to take full control of on my own. I would do what Jay Hunt had told me to do: play the long game, even though long-distance running probably wasn't quite what she'd had in mind. Neither she nor I had any idea of just how far her advice was going to take me. How many thousands of miles I would go on to run. How much inner confidence I would find along the way.

---

I never meant to end up on television. It was not on my to-do list as I was growing up. The limelight was something I avoided. As a teenager I felt awkward, often shy. I didn't like big groups. 'Speak, speak, I've never heard you speak,' ordered one of the 'cool' girls in front of the whole class when I was 14. I still remember exactly where I was sitting frozen under her glare, at a desk by the wall at the front of a third-floor classroom at Putney High School. Neither she, nor I, would have ever believed that not that many years later I would be speaking so much in public that she would have to switch me off when she'd had enough.

I fell into a job on screen by chance. Three years after I joined the BBC as a regional news trainee, I was working in Brussels as a producer, very much behind the scenes. It was 1994, the European Union had just been formed, and I was thriving on the thrill of my new journalism career.

'Would you be interested in a job in Leeds as a TV reporter with a view to becoming one of the presenters on BBC *Look North*?' That was the surprise question from the head of the regional news in Yorkshire, Martin Brooks, after I'd been in Brussels for more than a year. He'd chased me down after a big meeting at Television Centre in London with all the heads of the BBC's regional newsrooms. I was there telling them all about the Brussels operation and the stories we could provide for them over the coming months. 'Um thank you . . . but no. I don't think it's for me,' I said to Martin, a little confused. 'I mean I would like to do some reporting, but I really don't want to be a presenter.' It was the look afterwards on the faces of friends and colleagues, the jaws that dropped when I told them what had happened, that persuaded me to go back and at least have a chat. 'When a door opens, Sophie,' said the BBC's then North of England correspondent Kevin Bocquet, 'you must push it. You never know what's on the other side.'

'Do it. You'll be brilliant!' said my dad, always my greatest supporter. I wasn't sure. But I took the job. I was 27. It felt wrong to turn it down.

The learning curve was steep. A whole new world of studio lights, make-up and TV clothes that took me years to master. I had a constant feeling that I wasn't very good at it. After six months on the road reporting, which I loved, I was pushed into the studio. Every night as the *Look North* title music began and I heard the chatter of the production team in the gallery in my ear, my hands would start shaking. I didn't dare pick up a glass of water in case I spilt it all over my clothes. Then the red light would go on. And all I could think was, *Oh God! All those people out there! Hundreds of thousands of eyes just looking at me.* My brain would disengage from the words I was reading and before I knew it, I would be stumbling on a cue, heartbeat rising, the cold sweat of fear. I found it overwhelming at times. In the early days I tripped up on my words so much that apparently bets were placed in the studio gallery on how long it would be before I messed up my lines.

'You did often tell me you were really nervous, and I used to think, *Wow, I would never have known,*' says Mike McCarthy, my then co-presenter on *Look North*. 'I do remember you saying once that you felt sick while we were on air. I was just kind of sitting there thinking, *oh please, no, no, don't be sick. Not live!*'

I learnt to hide my fear, most of the time, like a young swan paddling frantically beneath the surface. I even started to enjoy the job. I liked the daily challenge, being part of a team tasked with getting a programme on air by the end of each day. I enjoyed the pressure, the buzz, the adrenaline, the last-minute changes before the red light went on at 6.30 p.m. every evening. But the limelight still made me feel uncomfortable. For someone who was now on TV most nights, I strangely didn't want to be looked at, scrutinised.

'Sophie – over here! Look this way! Look left! Give us a smile!' A bank of cameras, vulture-like, shouting out my name. Red-carpet appearances were a whole new experience when I moved to *Breakfast News* in London a few years later. Jeremy Bowen, a seasoned war reporter, was my co-presenter. We would be invited to film premieres, theatre premieres, award ceremonies. Jeremy had a lot more confidence than

I did. He would stride out in front of the wall of cameras with a huge smile and stand there basking in the photographers' lenses. I would scuttle off down the side of the carpet as fast as I could. Sometimes I dodged it completely, going around the back of them instead. Once safely inside, I would turn and watch Jeremy in front of the exploding camera flashes, glancing around, looking slightly confused, before realising that I had vanished from his side once again.

My visible discomfort at these red-carpet events landed me in the firm and freely roaming hands of Trinny Woodall and Susannah Constantine for their BBC One special 'What Not to Wear on the Red Carpet'. It was 2003 and Trinny and Susannah were huge stars, famous for prodding and poking their makeover victims and for their ability to transform what women wore.

I am not sure what possessed me to agree to a red-carpet makeover special. The BBC One bosses had asked me to do it and I had felt obliged to say yes. I was 34 and still finding my footing as I climbed the career ladder. Here was another open door to push on. Maybe this glam, assured TV duo could instil me with some of that confidence that still eluded me and teach me how to take the red-carpet scrutiny in my stride like others seemed to do with such ease.

We filmed the programme in the penthouse of a new tower block, the Montevetro, on the banks of the River Thames in Battersea. All glass and steel and London views. I arrived up there on the 17th floor, no make-up, dressed down in jeans and my favourite sheepskin coat and was immediately packed in tightly between Trinny and Susannah on a huge L-shaped sofa. Cornered. 'You've got tits, haven't you?' were pretty much Trinny's first words.

The researchers on the programme had searched high and low for photographs of me on a red carpet. They'd found none. Not a single one. A fact that rather pleased me and amazed them. So, they'd dispatched a producer to film me at a charity do I was hosting. And then they sat me down to watch it with them. 'You have a fabulous figure, you're not frumpy but that dress makes the top half of you look frumpy,' scolded willowy Trinny. 'And the art of walking in a high heel is very difficult, but you walk slightly like a carthorse,' she went on.

Their mission was to make me red-carpet ready, to be confident, to dress, walk and pose for the photographers. 'We've got to work on that moment when those photographers shout out at you. We've got to make sure you're wearing an appropriately conservative dress for your role as a newscaster but an appropriately sexy dress for you as a woman,' said Susannah. Sexy?! Alarm bells screeched in my head. I had only just started my new job with George Alagiah on the *Six O'Clock News* and now the Iraq War was looming. When I had been named as one of the new presenters on the evening news a few months earlier, the journalist Richard Ingrams had written in the *Observer*, 'Reading the news on television, which would once be a job entrusted to a battered-looking old party like Jeremy Bowen, will now be done by a sexy young blonde such as Sophie Raworth. When Mr Blair starts to bomb Baghdad, we shall be informed of the fact by a smiling bimbo with a perfect set of teeth.'

I worried constantly about being taken seriously but I had agreed to do *What Not to Wear* months ago and it was far too late to back out now. High up in the penthouse, I was manhandled by the duo as they pushed me into a mirrored room where they poked and prodded my body. They wanted me to stand there in my bra and pants. I flatly refused. 'I do the news!' I gasped. Instead, I was allowed to step in wearing jeans and a vest top before being analysed from every angle. D cups and a great arse that puts Jennifer Lopez to shame was their verdict. I was a little overweight. I did no exercise at all in those days and hardly thought about my shape or strength. I felt deeply uncomfortable being put on the spot. 'I'm not really bothered about my body. I don't really think about it that much,' I told them on camera, embarrassed. 'I just feel a bit odd talking about it in front of an awful lot of people.' I couldn't get out of that mirrored room fast enough. I was released on to a carpet that had been laid out in the penthouse, squeezed into tight dresses and taught how to look like I was gliding along in high heels.

I was being schooled for a red-carpet appearance at the 2003 TV BAFTA Awards at the London Palladium. The dress they chose for me was bright pink. No hiding. Tight, Ben de Lisi, clingy, vivid pink. 'I don't want to be unrecognisable. I don't want someone to say, "Who's that?"' I told them a little desperately. The awards were being held on Sunday 13 April. It was London Marathon day, a day of history as it turned out. 29-year-old Paula Radcliffe set a stunning world record finishing in 2 hours 15 minutes 25 seconds. Her incredible speed was all the talk in the hotel suite where I was being filmed that afternoon as the hair and make up team primped and preened me for my red carpet appearance. As I was driven in a Mercedes to the theatre, I gazed out at the packed pubs and bars full of exhausted-looking people wrapped in foil blankets with medals around their necks, never imagining for a moment that one day I would be one of them.

The red carpet outside the theatre was a blur of people, frocks, photographers, camera flashes and Trinny and Susannah standing at the end of it like anxious parents watching their child in a nativity play. I made it to the end, put my hand on my hip as they'd taught me to do, stood at an angle that would show off my waist and smiled before finally scurrying away. Ordeal over. 'What Not to Wear on the Red Carpet' was broadcast a week later on primetime BBC One. I refused to watch it and made my husband take me out for dinner instead. I had survived but I wasn't planning on going near any more red carpets for some time.

---

No one is watching when I step out of the door of our terraced house in London in 2006 for my first training run for the Great North Run. It's spring, early evening, cherry blossom on the tree-lined street. It is starting to warm up. My husband is too, bouncing from one foot to the other on the pavement, stretching his legs, getting ready for a quick run. I have pulled on my new Nike trainers, a pair of shorts and a really unflattering T-shirt and I'm on the pavement too now, copying Richard's energetic routine. I am about a stone overweight after having our second baby. I can't remember when I last tried running. I can't really remember when I last did any proper exercise at all.

'How far are we going?' I ask, trying not to sound nervous. 'Oh, only 3 miles or so. It's my usual short run. We could do the longer one if you want. But that's more than 5 miles around the river. Probably best to start with a short run and see how you go?' I nod in agreement, and we set off at a slow jog. *How hard can this be?* I keep thinking, clutching a bottle of water, as runners seem to do. 'You don't need to bring water,' Richard says, laughing. 'We are only going for half an hour!' I take it anyway. I feel like I may need it.

We cross over a couple of roads, passing people walking home from work, and already I'm enjoying the brief breaks when traffic lights mean we have to stop and wait for the cars. 'OK?' asks Richard, glancing over his shoulder. I make a strange sound as I nod my head. I'm finding it hard to speak because my lungs are feeling so tight. 'I just need to stop for a second,' I gasp, pulling up on the kerb. 'Just want a bit of water. My throat's feeling weirdly dry.' He looks bemused, jogging on the spot. We've only come half a mile. We run on again over a busy main road and down towards the Thames. I am sweating a lot now and out of breath. It's a horrible feeling, gasping for air, but my pride makes me try to keep up. Richard runs several times a week after work, just for fun. He's done a couple of marathons too. This really is just a walk in the park for him.

The River Thames is a welcome distraction. We turn on to a gravelly path running along the water under a leafy awning of plane trees that bring some much-needed shade. Across the river I can see the rowers lifting their boats high on their shoulders as they carry them back into the boathouses. The sun is going down, casting a golden glow on the white stone of a bridge up ahead. We dodge in and out of early evening strollers, families with small kids and friends chatting in pairs. Walking in this evening light looks a lot more pleasant than what I'm doing. Running hurts. I'm red-faced. My lungs feel like they're exploding. I am starting to feel a little panicky, though I don't say any of this now. How am I going to run 13 miles in Newcastle when I am struggling after less than 3?

I find a beginner's half marathon training plan. It gives me some structure. Week one: 2 miles on Tuesday, 3 miles on Thursday, 4 miles on Sunday. I can cope with that. The distance builds by a mile or two every week. Ten miles is the furthest I will run before the big day, which is three months away. Crucially, I tell people that I am going to run my first half marathon, because I know that once I have done that there will be no backing down.

With two children under the age of two, training time is a little limited. But I quickly discover how much more I seem to be able to fit into my day when I have some structure. Mornings are virtually impossible with a five-month-old baby to breastfeed. But by the time Richard is back from work, I'm ready to rush out of the door, thrusting small children at him as I go. The joy of running is that it doesn't take up that much time. Trainers on, into the street and I'm back within an hour. Yes, I still gasp for air and my lungs still feel like they're bursting. But now that I'm getting out there three times a week, I do start to realise that it's getting easier.

I return to work in the summer. Walking back into the newsroom where someone else is doing my old job sitting next to George is even harder than I expected. I smile a lot to mask the inner feeling of humiliation and try to breeze through it. But I feel anxious, strangely unanchored now. When Natasha is off work, other presenters are asked to do the *Six*, not me. A page has turned, and it seems I'm no longer part of that story. I worry about this. *Play the long game*, I keep thinking.

I run. I do exactly what my training plan tells me. Physically, it is tiring. Yet I start to discover an unexpected peace, time completely on my own away from small children, away from the worries of work. When I run, my mind seems to slow down. I am right here in the moment, away from it all. It is a release, unexpectedly calming.

At weekends, Richard tries to push me a little further than the week before. We pile both kids into a big double buggy and disappear off along the River Thames or do a lap of Richmond Park. Week by week we go farther. I find that I don't want to let him down. He seems so keen and proud that I am trying to do this. And then with a couple of weeks to go he drops a target time into the mix too. 'Let's try to do the Great North Run in under 2 hours,' he says, beaming.

On race day I am a bag of nerves. It is September 2006. Bill Turnbull, who I worked with for years on *Breakfast News*, is with us at the hotel in Gateshead where the elite athletes and the 'celebrity runners' are all staying. Bill is a seasoned long-distance runner and uses his humour and charm to calm me down. The Great North Run begins on a dual carriageway in Newcastle, a mile from the famous Tyne Bridge, which we will all run across as the Red Arrows roar overhead. More than 36,000 runners are moving towards the holding pens for each wave. I watch them from the comfort of our VIP bus as we pass through the crowds. A sea of people wrapped up in extra layers against the early morning cold, many of them sporting elaborate costumes, people dressed as beer bottles, fairies, superheroes. Towering above them all is a tall, bearded man in a vast pink dress. I wonder how on earth he is going to be able to run in that. Our bus passes through a barrier and down a slipway on to the dual carriageway, dropping us in front of the start line that is visible up ahead. In among the gaggle of celebrities and elite runners milling around there, I see Brendan Foster for the first time, the man whose fault it is that I'm standing here. 'Sophie! Welcome!' he shouts, waving to me above all the heads.

This is Brendan's race, and everybody knows it. He started it in 1981 when 12,000 people lined up to run the 'undulating' course from Newcastle to South Shields on the coast. He calls it 'undulating'. I call it hilly because that's exactly what it looks like to a runner who lives in a flat part of London. That said, 8 miles into the race and I feel like I'm coping. Richard is running with me, right next to me, quietly urging me on. We have already run this distance together in training. Two more miles and then I'll be in uncharted territory. *I'm doing all right*, I think to myself. *Good pace! We should get there in under 2 hours.*

'Agghhhhh!' I suddenly yelp in pain. Something has gone twang in my calf. We are going round a roundabout and I stop and limp to the side of the road, panic rising. 'You OK?' shouts Richard, who's seen it all happen. I hobble for a few paces to see if I can put my weight on it. I can but it hurts. 'Keep moving if you can. We can't stop now,' he says. 'It's going to seize up if you stop. Come on. It's only 3 miles until the end now.' I hesitate. Around us runners are streaming past, eyes fixed on the road ahead. 'Come on,' he shouts, louder this time. 'Dig your nails into your hand and KEEP RUNNING.' Then he disappears off ahead. I have no choice but to follow him, digging my nails into the palms of hands to try to distract my brain from my feet. It works. Ten minutes later and I'm not really thinking about my calf any more. I am having to concentrate more on the muscles in my thighs.

The last 2 miles of the Great North Run are brutal, particularly for a novice like me. There's a long, steep hill to climb that seems never-ending. 'Don't look up! Look at your feet,' Richard keeps saying. Then once we crest over the top of the hill with the North Sea suddenly in view, there's a steep drop down and my quads seem to go into shock. I can see the finish line at last, off in the distance along the coast road. The crowds get thicker and thicker, but the finish line doesn't seem to get any nearer. When we finally do get there a mile later, Richard, who doesn't enjoy the spotlight at all, peels off and goes in a different stream of runners so the TV cameras don't see him. We still finish in exactly the same time to the very second – 2 hours, 5 minutes, 11 seconds. Though to his amusement Richard gets listed in the results before me. 'Technically this means I beat you,' he says, laughing.

The BBC's Sue Barker is right by the finish line, broadcasting live on BBC One. I'm pulled up on to the platform for a post-race interview, my first running medal around my neck, a foil blanket around my shoulders and clutching a bottle of water that has been thrust into my hand. I feel utterly elated to have finished the race. I am buzzing after 13.1 miles, the furthest I have ever run. I did it. But I cannot imagine ever being able to turn around and run that distance again in what would be a full marathon. In fact, I have no desire to try.

---

My two-year-old son, Ollie, is milling about by my feet in the kitchen. He's a little fractious because I am distracted by the TV. It's April 2010 and the London Marathon is on. I've been watching all morning, hoping to catch a glimpse of Charlie Case, a mum I know from the kids' school, who out of nowhere suddenly announced she was running that day. *Charlie Case is running the marathon?!* I keep saying to myself over and over again. *Charlie? A whole marathon?* I didn't even know she'd been training! Charlie is 41 and just a month older than I am. A gorgeous blonde mother of two girls under seven, who has a huge gang of friends and parties a lot harder than I do. When on earth has she found the time to do marathon training? Now with three young children all under the age of six, I had rather given up on the idea of doing one. In the four years since that first race, I have run the Great North Run once more and finished in exactly the same time. I had convinced myself that my long-distance running days were over and I was already too old to take on a marathon. But Charlie, my age and out there running, has completely confused me.

I keep scanning the bobbing heads on TV looking for her. My ego has been a little pricked. If Charlie can run this, why can't I? Suddenly a tall, slim, leggy blonde comes into view. The TV cameras are on her as she makes a last dash for the finish line. It's not Charlie, but I do know her. 'Here comes the TV presenter Jenni Falconer,' says

Brendan Foster, sounding impressed, from the commentary box. 'I think that's 3 hours, 31 minutes – what a great time.' Jenni is beaming. She looks like she can't believe what she has just done. Sue Barker is there doing the BBC interviews, and I listen as Jenni tells her in breathy tones, with a huge beaming smile, about the unbelievable crowds on the streets and how delighted she is with her time. 'I owe it all to Karen Weir at Matt Roberts,' she gushes. Karen Weir. Matt Roberts. I grab a pencil and scribble it all down on a scrap of paper in the kitchen and start googling.

Karen Weir is a personal trainer. So is Matt Roberts. He owns a chain of gyms in London, and she works for him. I've managed to get through life without a trainer or a gym so far. But now perhaps it is time to dive in. I email Karen and tell her I want to run the marathon like Jenni, but I'm really worried I won't be able to do it. 'That feeling you had when you ran the Great North Run and thought that you could never turn round and run that again, that is a really common feeling,' she says when we finally meet. 'But everyone can do it. It's just that your brain gets you to the point that it needs to get you to. So, until now it has only ever needed to get you to 13.1 miles. Now it is going to be a matter of slowly building up that distance, increasing your long runs by no more than 10 per cent a week. The worst thing for most people is too much training, particularly if they're not elite athletes. If you've got a job, you've got kids, you cannot train realistically more than four or five times a week. And you don't need to. So, you can run a marathon on three runs a week. And you can fail to run a marathon because you've trained six times a week and absolutely knackered yourself.'

I sign up with Karen. She puts me through my paces, checking my strength, balance and fitness. I find I rather enjoy being tested. I am given a new training plan. This one is more demanding, with four to five runs a week. I print it out and stick it on the fridge. Day one says 'Rest'. I like that. I feel like I've been given my school timetable at the start of term and I have an exam to work for with 16 weeks to complete the job. 'Your biggest week is going to be three weeks before the London Marathon. You'll do about 40 miles that week, that's the absolute maximum,' Karen says.

It takes me a while to adjust to all of this exercise and training. It is not something I have done for decades. I didn't run much as a child. In fact, I did very little sport at all until I was 16. I left Putney High School in 1984 after my O-levels and went to St Paul's Girls' School in West London. St Paul's had a swimming pool with two diving boards. That's where I found myself, heart beating, one afternoon, waiting to show the parents and kids in the packed stands above what I could do. This was a school diving competition that I'd been told I should enter. The man judging it was an Olympic diver called Chris Snode. I had borrowed a white swimsuit from my friend Annabel for the occasion. My name was called, and I stepped onto the board.

I had been practising this dive for weeks, something I had had no idea I could do until the first swimming class here at my new school. I flew through the air, flattening my body against my thighs in pike position, before opening up again and slipping into the water in a straight line with just a small splash. Underwater, the muffled sound of applause from above before I burst back up through the surface and hauled myself out of the pool. Now people really were smiling, a few wide eyes as I looked around. 'Sophie,' beckoned one of my fellow divers as I grabbed my towel. 'Do you know that that swimsuit is see-through?' I looked down as my face flushed red and scuttled off into the changing room. I didn't win, but I was definitely noticed and not just for my friend's translucent white swimsuit. The next day, my teacher told me that Chris Snode had been in touch. He wanted me to go and meet Pete, one of the coaches at the Highgate Diving Club who trained some of the British diving squad.

I started training with the team on Tuesdays and Thursdays after school at 6.30 p.m. – 2-hour sessions at Barnet Copthall swimming pool in North London, just off the M1, a very long way from my family home in Twickenham in South West London. I did my homework in the car on the long journey back. Weekends would be trampolining in the morning, then diving in the afternoon. It was a huge commitment given I was doing my A-levels. But for the first time in my life, I discovered the joy of training for a sport that I could potentially be good at. I felt a sense of belonging, the thrill of progression and the support that came from a diverse group of people from all walks of life, all united by the desire to perfect the art of flying through the air into the pool as gracefully as we could.

Among my new teammates was Jay, an 18-year-old beautiful diver with a thick head of dark hair, who travelled for training all the way from Great Yarmouth, where he worked on his parents' market stall. Vince, who we all called Ginge because of his hair, was 19, a gymnast who'd decided to take his acrobatics into the pool. And Lea was an American who lived in London, a year younger than I was.

We spent hours together by the pool in swimsuits and Speedos, diving, chatting, sparring, training. Ginge and Jay teased me mercilessly most of the time, endless ribbing about being posh. 'Me and Jay were like little schoolboys when you came along. You always used to tell us you wanted to be a journalist, you wanted to do documentaries and that,' Ginge says when I track him down again 40 years later. 'Me and Jay used to take the mickey out of you all the time and call you the posh girl. I remember saying to you that you should be on the BBC and read the 6 o'clock news because you were so posh. It's amazing how that's come true, isn't it?' he laughs.

The training and my A-levels became too much. I lost touch with them all completely when I quit diving a year later. But one day, many years later, I bumped into Lea in London. 'How is everyone? Do you know what they're all doing?', I asked, delighted to see her again. 'Well, Ginge is a stuntman doing lots of Hollywood films. He has done really well for himself,' she told me. 'And Jay, you know what he's doing, obviously.' 'No, I've no idea,' I replied, confused. 'What's Jay up to?' 'Jay. Jason. Jason Statham, Hollywood star,' she laughed. I couldn't believe it. It had never occurred to me that the teenager I spent a year with poolside in Speedos was now the 'hardman' actor in Guy Ritchie's films. He had had loads of hair when I knew him for starters. Though now that she mentioned it, I had always thought I did recognise his voice from somewhere.

St Paul's also had an athletics track. For one summer only I trained and competed with the school team, racing the 400 metres. I was good. I discovered I could run. I was fast. But A-levels got in the way of that too, and I never went back. It would be 20 years before I trained for any kind of sport again.

---

Marathon training is far more intense and time-consuming than anything I have done before. It takes my body time to adapt. I discover muscles and tendons that I never knew I had. My *gluteus medius* in my hip, rather important as it turns out; hamstrings, which are vital; my iliotibial band (ITB) that runs down the side of each thigh and pulls hard on my knee if it's too tight. *Am I damaging my body?* I keep wondering. *Am I hurting my knees?* I am introduced to foam rollers that I sit or lie on to smooth out the knots of muscle in my calves and thighs. I have my first sports massage. It is so excruciating that I resort to breathing techniques that I was taught for childbirth just to get through it. 'Don't worry,' says Karen repeatedly. 'You've done no exercise for decades! Your body is just adapting to the new load. It's getting used to it. It'll get easier as you get stronger.' I try ice baths too, though I can't quite bring myself to go full ice. Instead, I sit in cold water in our bath, in a fleece and bobble hat, and shiver for 10 whole minutes. There's a mental stress, too, which is unexpected. I'm never quite sure whether to run if something feels a bit sore. I set off on one long Sunday run after days of niggles and 20 paces in I am forced to turn back. It hurts too much. I feel stressed because now I will miss my long run this week. It won't be ticked off on my training plan on the fridge. Am I going to fall behind? Will I have done enough training to get to the marathon start line? I text Bill Turnbull, who's well versed in the odd injury, for a bit of advice and reassurance. 'You are suffering from MAD,' he texts straight back. 'Marathoner's Anxiety Disorder. Don't worry about it. Rest. Enjoy it.'

My long runs every Sunday get longer and longer as the weeks pass by. Karen tells me how many minutes to run rather than how many miles. We start with 75 minutes and increase it a bit each week. The most I will have to do is 190 minutes, three weeks before race day. Somehow, time over distance is more manageable psychologically. 'It's just about time on your feet,' she keeps telling me.

With five weeks to go, my longest training run is a 20-mile race around the Dunsfold Aerodrome in Surrey called the Spitfire 20. I wake up early feeling nervous and then remember why. My head fills with all kinds of excuses not to go. My three-year-old son has a cough. It's pouring with rain. It's a long way to drag the family. I'm not feeling great. I suggest to Richard that we stay at home and I'll do a 20-mile run on my own along the river. 'Not an option!' he replies, smiling, and walks out of the room.

Two hours later I am standing with hundreds of other people in the rain on the disused airfield near Cranleigh, where the BBC films *Top Gear*, half hoping that Jeremy Clarkson and the Stig might emerge and sweep me off for a test drive. Instead, my husband appears and pushes me towards the start line.

Karen has given me strict instructions to run the first 15 miles of the race at a 9.5-minute per mile pace, before pushing harder in the last 5 miles to the finish. I tuck in with some runners who are a similar pace and dip in and out of their chatter. At the halfway point my parents suddenly loom into view on the side of the airfield in the heavy rain. They have driven here from London to watch me; it's the first time they have ever seen me run. I wave at them madly. They both burst into tears, which is disconcerting.

At 15 miles, as I'm about to up the pace, I catch up with a man in a fluorescent T-shirt and for a mile or two we seem to be playing tag, overtaking each other again and again. Finally, we start chatting. He is an actor, as it turns out, who's just been playing an 'upper-class pirate' alongside Johnny Depp in *Pirates of the Caribbean*. And so I dash towards Dunsfold Aerodrome with a posh pirate and see my parents, husband and kids all going wild on the finish line. The last big run before London is done.

The training takes over my life. I become obsessed. The producers on the *One O'Clock News* team get so bored of hearing me talk about it all the time that they set new rules. I'm allowed to mention the word 'running' once a day. Any more than that and I have to go and buy all the teas. It gets expensive.

That doesn't stop me mentioning it to the Prime Minister when I find myself in the Drawing Room in Downing Street with a fortnight to go. Prince William and Kate Middleton are getting married on 29 April 2011, 12 days after the marathon. I've been asked to do a 'quick turnaround' documentary about the young couple and the history of British royal weddings.

I arrive in Downing Street for my interview with David Cameron, who is going to talk about royal weddings and his thoughts on Kate and William's big day. You can't take mobile phones into Number 10. You have to leave them in numbered pigeonholes in the hall by the famous front door. I've become highly superstitious with the marathon looming. I see potential signs and predictions in everything I do. So here I am, staring at a whole lot of numbered pigeonholes, convinced that the one I choose could have a direct bearing on marathon day. I hover there for far too long. Should I choose a number in the 30s? This would mean a sub-4-hour finish. Or is that a bit optimistic? Maybe I should go for something in the low 40s, which would mean I'd finish it in under 4 and a half hours. I opt for pigeonhole 40, which I decide means 4 hours. If I make it round in that time, I will be euphoric.

David Cameron sweeps into the Drawing Room and takes his seat. I've already clocked from newspaper stories that he goes running with Matt Roberts, who owns the gyms where Karen works. 'Good to see you,' he says, shaking my hand. 'How are you?' 'I'm exhausted. I'm about to run the London Marathon. I've been training really hard,' I say. I catch my producer's eye. Too much marathon talk already. I can see what's coming. They're going to make me buy the teas again. Actually, they'll probably upgrade it to a huge round of drinks in the pub now. I pull myself together, the camera goes on and we start talking about what I am really here for: the Royal wedding.

This documentary means I am also spending rather a lot of time filming pieces to camera on The Mall, on the very spot where the marathon finish line is about to be installed.

I find myself welling up at the idea of running down here in less than a fortnight to the sound of a roaring crowd.

In the end, though, there was of course no euphoria for me on 17 April 2011. After all that training, after all that obsessive chat about training, I just felt shame and was embarrassed that I had blacked out and limped across the finish line hours after I had expected to.

Among the many messages I get in the days after the marathon is an email from a professor of sport at the University of Bedfordshire, John Brewer. He explains in great detail what probably happened to me, saying I had no doubt overheated and pushed on when I should have slowed down. He had done the same thing himself in his first marathon in 1982, he tells me, and he had collapsed near Big Ben. He hadn't finished the race. Instead, he had woken up in hospital 24 hours later in a pretty bad state. 'I found that the best way to put the record straight,' he wrote, 'was to run another marathon, and prove that I could do it without similar problems.' 'That's exactly what I have already decided to do,' I type back. 'But I'm not sure how I am going to break it to my parents.'

# 3

## *Mission to the Stars*

With 2 miles to go until the finish line of the 2017 Chicago Marathon, my friend Susie Chan starts shouting my name. 'I feel like I am going to pass out, Soph,' she gasps. 'Whatever happens, do not let them carry me off the course. Promise me? Even if I faint, do not let them take me out of the race. I have to finish this. We've got to finish it together.'

I move in closer to her. Her husband, Shaun, is flanking her on the other side. We have slowed down a lot. I don't think I have ever had to stop and wait for Susie to catch up before. She looks terrible. She has been coughing violently for days now, so much so that at times she has had to hold on to something to stay upright. If this had been any other marathon, she would have pulled out. But the Chicago Marathon is the end of our three-and-a-half-year journey around the world together in pursuit of a 'Six Star Medal'. We have to get to the end.

---

After the drama of my debut at London in 2011, I did of course go back the following year and I finished the marathon under the magic 4-hour barrier, in 3 hours, 56 minutes. 'Here comes Sophie Raworth,' cried out Brendan Foster on TV from the BBC commentary box as he spotted me on a camera running down The Mall. 'Sophie Raworth is without doubt the most improved athlete of the ENTIRE field,' he said with a laugh as I shaved 2 hours and 26 minutes off last year's personal best. The marathon bug had bitten. I discovered I loved the training, the discipline and the structure that it brought to my life as well as the realisation that despite being in my early 40s, I was getting faster, I wasn't too old. My confidence grew too. People around me seemed visibly impressed by what I was doing. I quietly basked in the glow of their kind words. After a few years of being a little unsure of my footing at work, running had made me feel steadier on my feet and in my mind. *Could I go faster?* I kept asking myself. *How much faster could I go if I put in a little more time?* I decided to find out. I shaved off more than 10 minutes in my third London Marathon, finishing in just under 3 hours, 45 minutes. 'That's a Boston qualifying time,' a friend told me, delighted. 'You should apply! Try to get in!'

The Boston Marathon is the oldest annual marathon in the world. It dates back to 1897 and you have to qualify to be able to run it. I was very new to this world of marathons but quickly realised this race was something of a runners' Mecca, something I needed to tick off. The qualifying times work on a sliding scale, so the older you are, the easier it is to get in. I needed to beat 3 hours, 45 minutes for a place but there was no guarantee. Only the fastest in each group would be selected and I had only just made the time with seconds to spare. I decided to give it a go anyway. To my surprise, I did get in. But that left me with a dilemma. I had already qualified for a place in the London 2014 marathon, through their 'Good For Age' scheme which gives automatic entry every year to 6000 runners who are the fastest in their age groups. The Boston Marathon was eight days after London. Two marathons in eight days? It sounded crazy.

I took to Twitter. 'I have places for both the London and Boston marathons. They're eight days apart. Which one should I do?!' My Twitter feed lit up with plenty of advice, mostly to ditch London and go to Boston. Then up popped a runner called Susie Chan. 'Do both,' she wrote, 'I am!'

The first time I met Susie in the flesh was thousands of feet above the Atlantic, on a British Airways plane to Boston. Shoulder-length dark hair, half Hong Kong Chinese, a huge smile, a bundle of energy and enthusiasm. We connected instantly. She was in her mid-30s, a curator at the British Museum and a single mother, who not so long ago had been partying, unfit and smoking. Like me, she had stumbled into a running addiction later in life. Unlike me, she had rocketed from a half marathon wearing plimsolls to the legendary 150-mile Marathon des Sables race across the Sahara Desert in Morocco, which she had run just 18 months later. Her can-do, will-do, never-give-up spirit infected me at once.

I shared a cab into Boston with Susie and her cousin Samantha. I had travelled out there on my own, leaving my husband and three young kids at home. Richard would have loved to have come and run it with me. But an injury to his foot more than a decade ago now had made long-distance running too painful. I was feeling both brave and a little anxious about running this marathon alone. My legs were still tired and stiff from the London Marathon, which I had run a few days before, and it was only three years since I had collapsed in the race. It still made me nervous. But already in Boston I was starting to gather a small band of runners around me. By the time I left that city I would have acquired a whole gang.

Boston was awash with the colour orange and high on emotion in the days running up to the marathon. There were thousands of lean, fit-looking people wandering the streets in trainers, proudly dressed in the official 2014 Boston Marathon kit, which was an almost fluorescent tangerine colour that year. There was an added layer of intensity. This would be the first marathon since the terrorist attack at the Boston Marathon the year before, when two home-made devices had been left in backpacks among the spectators on the finish line. They exploded 12 seconds apart, killing three people and injuring more than 250 others. The race had been halted with thousands of runners still out on the course. There was something particularly brutal about targeting the running community, people who had trained for months to complete the distance, cheered on by family and friends. Twelve months later and Boston was once again a sea of runners. Now there was an air of defiance and a determination to run again. The words 'Boston Strong' and 'We Run As One' were emblazoned all over the city.

I felt unsettled for another reason too. Three days before I had flown out here, George Alagiah, my friend and former co-presenter on the *Six O'Clock News*, had texted me when I was at home. 'Sophie, I know you're on holiday, but could we have a chat?' he wrote. I called him straight away and in his soft and measured tones he began telling me that after months of stomach problems, which he had put down to foreign travel and some dodgy food, he had been diagnosed with bowel cancer. It had spread to his liver. It was stage 4. He was only 58 years old. I sank down on to the floor in my bedroom, wedged between the bed and the walls, my knees hunched up to my chest and listened, tears in my eyes, trying hard not to let him hear me crying.

George and his family had become close friends in the years since we had first worked together. He had invited Richard and me to his 50th birthday party, some of just a handful of friends who were included in the large family gathering in a marquee in his back garden. The party was on the day I was due to give birth to our second child. When she finally arrived two weeks later, we named her Georgia, after him, one of the kindest, most decent and thoughtful people I knew. Now here he was, eight years later, telling me that the situation wasn't looking good. 'Let's just hope I'm around and we're having this conversation in five years' time,' he said before hanging up.

Jet lag meant I was up before dawn in Boston. I took my laptop downstairs and sat drinking tea in the hotel's deserted foyer. I decided to set up a charity fundraising page for George. He had just gone public with his news. The response was almost instant. Within hours, thousands of pounds had been donated by complete strangers, people who welcomed George into their sitting rooms every night. 'Running For George' gave me a whole new purpose, a reason to finish this race however much it would hurt my already weary legs.

After breakfast, I arranged to meet Susie at my hotel and we wandered up to the Expo centre to pick up our race numbers. Inside the vast hall, among all the stands selling marathon kit, shoes and energy bars, was a large area all in blue with a big shiny medal in a glass box in the middle. We peered in. The Abbott World Marathon Majors Six Star Medal was huge. We'd never heard of it before. But this medal was made up of six circles for its six marathons – London, Boston, Berlin, Chicago, New York City and Tokyo – with the circles depicting each city all welded together. On the walls around us was a 'Hall of Fame', the names of just under 400 people from all over the world who had already run those marathons and achieved their Six Star status. Susie and I studied the names intently. Only 98 of them were women and just a handful of them were British. We looked at each other, grinning. 'Let's do it!' we said.

The next morning, on race day, a fleet of hundreds of yellow school buses were lined up all over the city centre. The kind of buses you see in American movies, the ones I grew up watching on the Charlie Brown cartoons as a child. The fun of getting into one for the first time distracted me a little from the fear of what was ahead. The Boston Marathon is a point-to-point race that starts out in Hopkinton, Massachusetts, and ends back in the city centre. Susie was a faster runner than me. She was in an earlier wave and so she'd set off for the start of the race already. I boarded my allotted bus with a woman I knew from my local parkrun in Richmond. I was rather in awe of Jacquie Millet, a psychotherapist by trade who'd quickly learnt a lot about marathon running. She had only started running a few years earlier after a cancer scare when she was 57. Now, four years later, she had already completed 43 marathons as well as a 55-mile ultramarathon called Comrades Marathon in South Africa. She had also, like me, run the London Marathon eight days ago in under 4 hours, in almost exactly the same time as I had. On the bus ride out to the start line, we decided we would run Boston together. I felt a little safer by her side.

The drive out to the Athletes' Village in Hopkinton seemed endless. The yellow bus convoy stretched out along the highway as far as the eye could see. The journey felt like 50 miles, not 26.2. By the time we arrived, the first wave in the race was about to start. Tannoys were calling all the fastest runners into their pens. I headed for the huge queues at the portaloos, long lines of people jiggling around dressed in old clothes, even bin bags, to keep warm. Marathon portaloos were a whole new experience for me. A smelly baptism of fire that I had so far managed to avoid, thanks to my repeated invitations to the VIP hospitality area at the London start line. That was a world of 'posh loos' with red carpet, flushing water, rolls of loo paper and no queues. Here the lines of hundreds of runners snaked out across the muddy grass. Once I finally got inside the portaloo, I made the mistake of looking down. No running water; no water at all. Just a foul growing mound of smelly human excrement and white loo paper piling up in a deep hole in the ground. I got out as fast as I could.

The temperature was warming up as we walked the half mile or so to the start, showing our race numbers to the marshals who were checking we were in the right pen. I was getting increasingly anxious about overheating again and was glad to have Jacquie by my side. Boston is a notoriously hilly race. It doesn't let you settle. The first few miles are downhill and surprisingly steep, working your quads hard. From then on, the rolling hills seem never-ending and running down them starts to hurt as much as running up. The middle miles of a marathon get me every time – you're far enough in that you feel tired but still far enough from the finish to wonder how on earth you're going to get there without stopping. It's at this point in the Boston Marathon that you reach the Newton Hills – four of them in quick succession from miles 16 to 21. The final one in the pack that hits you at mile 20 is the infamously named Heartbreak Hill, a steep half-mile climb that gets all the muscles in your legs screaming. It is both a physical and mental battle to the top.

Jacquie and I stayed together throughout. The huge crowds urged us on. Jacquie was wearing a Union Jack running vest and people shouted and cheered at us, thanking us for travelling so far to be there after the tragedy of last year. Heartbreak Hill did indeed almost break me, but I ground it out, looking at my feet rather than searching for the top, until I reached the signs people were holding aloft saying 'You're Over The Hill' and 'Heartbreak Hurts But You'll Get Over It'. That made me smile. We crested the peak and rolled down another hill towards the Boston skyscrapers and the finish.

With 4 miles to go, I grabbed water and walked through a drinks station. A big mistake. Once you stop running, it's hard to start again. Jacquie glanced over her shoulder. 'Come on, keep running,' she shouted, waving me on. I struggled to get going again. Everything hurt and I was hot now. Jacquie stopped and waited. 'Go ahead, I'm going to walk a bit. I can't do it,' I said. She looked at me sternly, this petite, dark-haired woman who was 16 years older than I was, and said quietly, 'Sophie, anyone can run a marathon. But it's when the going gets really tough that you find out just what you're made of. And I know you can do this. So come on. We are going to keep running.' And off she went, knowing I would have to follow, clinging on to her heels.

We crossed the finish line together in just over 4 hours. My head started spinning. As we made our way towards the exit, I was struggling to walk and then my legs seemed to be giving way under me. One of the race marshals spotted me and pushed a first-aider towards me with a wheelchair. Once again, I was carted off to a medical tent. At least this time I had crossed the finish line first.

Once back on my feet, the first person I called was George Alagiah. Wrapped up in a foil blanket with my medal around my neck, I stood on Boston Common with thousands of other shattered but smiling people and told him about the race, about how hard it had been and that when I didn't think I could run another step, I had trailed behind Jacquie, reminding myself about all the operations and treatment he was about to go through. George couldn't believe how much money I had already raised in just one day and had been reading some of the messages of support on my fundraising page from friends, colleagues and BBC viewers who were all so shocked about his cancer.

I limped slowly back to my hotel, which was close enough to the finish line to have become a magnet for my newly acquired running friends. At the entrance, staff were handing out laurel wreaths, crowning exhausted runners as they thrust free smoothies at us. Susie was already there, lounging on a big sofa, ordering copious amounts of chips. Jacquie joined our growing gang, as did another Brit, Tim, who Susie and I had met the day before when he asked us for directions to the Expo. A tall, fast runner called Ben, who also worked in TV, came too. What none of us knew as we gathered that day in our post-Boston glow was that in the years to come, we would continue running many more miles together all over the world.

My flight home early the next day was painful. Sore legs jammed under a seat in economy for seven hours, my medal still around my neck. One of the British Airways cabin crew recognised me as I shuffled on board. My fundraising efforts for George had been reported in the news. 'He seems like such a lovely man,' the air steward said as I boarded. As we waited on the tarmac before taxiing, he walked down the aisle scanning the seats, a paper cup in his hand. 'Madam, here's that apple juice you asked for,' he said, thrusting it at me. I looked around, confused. 'Um, I didn't order any apple juice. I don't think it's for me,' I said as I smiled back. 'Yes you did,' he insisted, thrusting it back at me again with a wink. I took it and had a sip. Fizz. Golden bubbles. By the time I landed in London, still wearing my medal, I'd been handed so much 'apple juice' that I had a hangover.

A week later George started chemotherapy. I had brought back T-shirts for him and his wife Franny from America with 'Boston Strong' emblazoned across the front. I gave him my highly prized Boston Marathon medal too, with a note saying: 'The hardest thing I've ever got through physically – so I reckon you should have this for a while.

Hope it does the job.' On the day his cancer treatment began, Franny texted me a photo of George lying on a hospital bed, thumbs up to the camera, smiling, with my Boston medal around his neck. 'Boston Strong,' she wrote – a motto that the three of us would keep using for the rest of his life.

Two years later, when George went into remission, he sent my medal back to me, framed with a photo of him and Franny in the middle wearing their Boston T-shirts and the words, 'You helped us to stay strong.' It's on the wall in my kitchen, by the fridge. It's still one of the first things I see every day when I go to get milk for my cup of tea in the morning. It always makes me smile.

George returned to work in the autumn of 2015 after 18 months of major operations and a lot of chemotherapy. He came back just as I was flying off to New York on a mission to bag my third World Marathon Majors star. I opened up my 'Running for George' fundraising page again and thousands more pounds poured in. George was really nervous about going back on air, but he did it beautifully, with no fanfare or fuss, just a simple 'It's good to be back' as he signed off at the end of the programme. 'I almost cried,' I texted him after watching from home. 'Wonderful to see you on the tele. And a faultless performance too. You are "trending" on Twitter mate! #bostonstrong.' He replied hours later: 'So glad I've got that first one out of the way. Bostonstrong indeed. Little did we know it would become the motif of the last 18 months. Off to bed – shattered but utterly content xx.'

Boston Strong were two words we continued to use over and over again in the years that followed. I'd type them to George and to Franny every time he was going in for another operation, more scans or extra chemo rounds that had been ordered. If it was a particularly dangerous moment, I would send him a photo of my medal that he had framed as well. When I scroll back now through all the messages we exchanged over the years, I can still hear his voice, loud and clear in my head. I could always tell when he was coming out of a chemo fog because he'd text me straight after the *Six* with his thoughts on the bulletin and the stories of that day. Ironically it was George's illness that had put me on a new steadier footing at work. He had become the sole anchor on the *Six* after Natasha Kaplinsky had swapped the BBC for Channel 5. Increasingly I was being asked to fill in for him while he was off being treated for cancer. I had been brought back into the fold but for the saddest of reasons.

I sent George a photo of my framed medal and typed 'Boston Strong' on 1 July 2023. He was by now gravely ill in hospital. It was the last message we ever exchanged. Three weeks later, on 24 July, Franny texted me: 'Your beloved friend and my beloved husband died this morning. All was peaceful and we were all with him.' George was 67 years old.

I had to dig my nails extra hard into my hands that day, the trick my husband had taught me years earlier during my first half marathon. Only a few of us at the BBC knew how ill George had been in those last few weeks. He was much-loved and respected at work, a gentleman who was kind, unfailingly polite, always diligent and who loved being in the newsroom, loved the banter and the teamwork. He was a great journalist of course, award-winning, one of the best of his generation. He cared deeply about the *Six* and *Ten*, and those who worked with him cared deeply about him. I had been quietly working on a special TV tribute for George for more than a month, ever since Franny had told me it was touch and go.

Only a few weeks earlier, just before he took a turn for the worse, George had invited me for 'lunch' at the hospital where he was being treated, though he wasn't eating. Instead, drugs were being dripped into him. They were so toxic that the nurse was wearing goggles and gloves and arm protectors to stop her being burnt. I couldn't imagine what they were doing to his insides. He wanted to tell me that he had decided to pull back a little on the chemo. He talked of choice and control and more good times over bad. He'd had at least five major operations and around 200 rounds of chemotherapy. He said he had lost count. And yet he bore it all with such good grace. He was often in pain – yet I never heard him complain. He was endlessly positive and optimistic. When George was first diagnosed with stage 4 cancer in 2014, he wasn't expected to live for more than five years. But somehow, he had defied the statistics. Now though, almost 10 years later, he knew that he wouldn't be returning to work. He did want to do one more thing, he said. His plan was to come back to the Six as soon as he was feeling a little better, do an interview with me and then turn to the camera one more time and sign off. A final goodbye to an audience who had been watching him for more than 20 years.

In the end he didn't get to do that. Instead, we did it for him. One of our editors, Alice Young, who I knew George was really fond of, spent days putting together a montage of George in his own words. He had done very few interviews about having cancer since he was diagnosed almost a decade ago. He was a private man, but he also didn't think people would be that interested and was always surprised when something he did say about his illness landed him on the front pages of newspapers. We pulled together clips of George talking about living with cancer from a couple of podcasts he had agreed to do and found an interview he had done on camera for a doctors' conference about what it was like living with cancer. Alice spent hours lacing it all together with footage of him.

The news of George's death was going to be made public at noon on the day he died. With half an hour to go, the *Six* and *Ten* team were called to an urgent meeting in the newsroom. Paul Royall, our former editor, who had been a good friend of George's and had worked with him for more than a decade, told everyone the news. People sat stunned. There was silence. Shock. Many had thought he would come back to work again because he had done, so many times before. George's great friend, the correspondent Allan Little, who had worked with him in the BBC's South Africa bureau for many years, went on air within minutes of his death being announced. We all willed him on, amazed that he managed to hold it together. Clive Myrie's voice cracked an hour later on the *News at One*. I watched it all from the newsroom in the *Six O'Clock News* presenter's chair where George had sat so many times. I was presenting the news that night. George's face was now on every TV monitor in the newsroom, his death was being reported on every channel.

'Am I going to be able to do this on air tonight?' I asked my husband on the phone. 'Am I going to get through it without crying?' 'Yes – you absolutely are. Of course you are. You are doing it for George. Just think of that,' he said.

The studio gallery was packed that evening. Our editor, John Neal, several producers, the usual gallery team and many of the BBC's most senior bosses came down. I knew they were all there, but it was weirdly quiet. Just the voice of our director, Ryan, talking to me through my earpiece. Steady and reassuring. I went into the studio on my own half an hour early and read the words I had written over and over again out loud, hoping that the more I said them, the easier it would be to say them on air without breaking down. I stood there in the studio listening to the countdown as we were about to go live, heart hammering, and as the red light came on and the camera moved towards me, I glanced up at this huge image of George with a beaming smile in the big tower next to me and I couldn't help but smile back. It was lovely to have him right there again beside me.

At the end of the bulletin, we returned to the news of George's death. I explained that we were ending the programme with him in his own words. My voice cracked a little. I dug my nails into the back of my hand even harder. I could see the marks on my skin for hours afterwards. Then the film Alice had put together began. No one spoke. There was complete silence as George's voice filled the studio again, describing the moment he was told he had cancer. 'At first when you're told, you don't know how to respond, and it took me a while to understand what I needed to do,' he explained. 'For me, I had to get to a place of contentment and the only way I knew how to do that was literally to look back at my life… I have gotten to a place to see life as a gift. Rather than kind of worrying about when it's going to end and how it's going to end, I've got to a place where I can see it for the gift it is. I feel that gift keenly every morning.'

Afterwards the whole team went to a rooftop bar by the BBC and stood on a balcony, telling stories about George as we looked out at the sweeping vast views of London around us. I sent a photo to Franny of all of us raising a toast to our great friend.

---

After the Boston Marathon, my life had taken on a new rhythm. I stopped pounding the tarmac in London. On Sunday mornings I started heading out of the city early to meet up with my newfound running friends, Susie, Tim and Susie's husband, Shaun. With them I discovered a different kind of running out on the trails as well as an unexpected new level of trust with people I had only just met. They could tell from my stride and the number of kit faffing stops what kind of mood I was in, how my week had been. No questions were asked; there was no need to discuss anything. We just powered on or eased up depending on how we felt. People of all ages and backgrounds out there together, one foot in front of the other. No one asked me about my job or treated me any differently because I was on TV. I was just another runner. We didn't discuss careers and work. It took me years to find out what some people actually did when they took their trainers off. Yet I knew everything there was to know about their fastest times, their running niggles and their race plans and dreams for the months ahead. We became invested in each other's running successes – from parkrun PBs to tracking marathons online, willing each other on and cheering from afar.

I found a new easy kind of camaraderie that required no front. As my fitness improved, I pushed myself harder, I suffered more. Out there in the elements, I felt stripped back to my core, the real me, no room for pretence. Away from the TV studios and my job in which I always had to appear in control, I couldn't hide my limits, my weaknesses. But slowly I learnt to push at them, to ride them out, discovering along the way that my body could keep going when my mind was saying otherwise. We ran in sunshine, in torrential rain, through mud, in snow. I found freedom, endurance and the sense of a deeper connection to the earth as my feet pounded the trails.

I was getting stronger, too. The cycles of marathon training that I had been doing since I first started more than four years ago were paying off. My body was indeed adapting to the load. My muscles were learning what to do. I was leaner. I felt more sure of myself, both physically and mentally. I walked taller on red carpets now, no longer trying to camouflage myself by dressing down or scuttling around the back of photographers. 'That's not Sophie Raworth, is it?' I heard one photographer almost gasp as I strode towards a bank of cameras in a clingy long Donna Karan evening dress. 'Yup! It's me,' I said, laughing. I felt great.

---

With London and Boston ticked off, New York was next in my sights. New York City Marathon is huge. More than

50,000 runners wind their way from Staten Island through New York's five boroughs, ending up in Central Park. I'd got into the race on the ballot in 2015 but Susie hadn't, so I went with some of my parkrun friends, Sally and Mike. New York is held in the first week of November and it is notoriously cold. I made the whole experience so much harder by being late and unprepared. We were up before dawn to get the ferry to Staten Island. Thousands of runners dressed in throwaway extra layers poured on to the boats that shuttled us across the water, past the Statue of Liberty, to the Staten Island ferry terminal from where we would get the bus.

The marathon starts on the Verrazzano-Narrows Bridge that connects Staten Island to the New York borough of Brooklyn, a mile-long double-decked suspension bridge that for decades was the longest in the world. The Athletes' Village is beneath it in Fort Wadsworth, which is totally exposed and can be icy cold at that time of year. Sally, Mike and I thought we were being clever by hunkering down on the warm floor of the ferry terminal with hundreds of other runners. It wasn't even 8 a.m. I had almost two hours to wait before my run began. We kept warm for a while before heading out to board one of the buses that would take us to the start. That's when I spotted the traffic jams and realised that the start was 9 miles away. My panic began. The buses were travelling in convoy and crawling through the narrow streets ahead. Sally and Mike were in the wave after me, so had more time on their hands.

When the bus finally disgorged us all out into the Athletes' Village, I had less than 30 minutes to find a loo and get into my starting pen before it closed. I waved goodbye to my friends and tore off through the crowds, trying to find the right wave. It was divided up into three colours and six corrals. I was so flustered that I kept running the wrong way, using up precious energy that I had been trying to conserve for the race. Above me on the bridge, Frank Sinatra was in full voice, belting out his iconic tribute to New York as ticker tape rained down on the runners already on their way.

I darted this way and that, showing my race number to marshals who kept pointing me in different directions. Then suddenly I popped out on to a side road on the bridge and to my surprise realised that I was in the race and about to cross the start line. I had no time at all to calm my mind and focus on the 26.2-mile run ahead. Instead, with runners surging along behind me, I struggled out of my throwaway extra layers, chucked them on the side of the road, checked that my energy gels were all securely tucked into my race belt, started my running watch and stepped over the start line.

This was my first marathon entirely on my own. There were several people I knew running but only one in the same wave as me – Tim, our Boston friend – and I'd left myself no time to find him. Marathons are a mental challenge as much as a physical one, as I was about to discover. I knew friends, including Susie, would be tracking me from home and I felt under pressure to finish in under 4 hours.

The start was spectacular. Helicopters hovered low. The sky was azure blue. A cold wind blew across the bridge. Tugs below us in New York Bay threw out huge plumes of water, adding to the carnival atmosphere. My legs were feeling sluggish already after my scramble to find the start and the rising road on the bridge wasn't helping. I had imagined New York to be a flattish race. Quite the opposite. I should have done my research. It was the hilliest of all the Abbott World Marathon Majors, almost 1000 feet (more than 300m) of elevation, thanks to the five bridges you have to cross, and right now I was on the steepest. The crowds started thickening as we ran on. I kept a steady pace and tried to distract myself by taking in the sights around me. The course was much tougher than I'd expected, rolling hills and bridges, and I was struggling to harness my mind. At mile 15 there was another long climb on to the Queensboro Bridge, a famous part of the course because it's the third bridge and the one that finally takes you into Manhattan and the last 10 miles of the race. I knew my husband and his friend Gavin were waiting down there on First Avenue to cheer me on. I could hear the wall of noise long before I could see the faces. As we turned on to it, the shouts and claxons hit us all. I scanned the people with their signs and banners to find Richard and Gavin. When I finally saw them, I just stopped. My husband gave me a huge hug. 'I'm having an awful time,' I moaned. 'I've still got such a long way to go.' Richard, who'd run the New York City Marathon many years before, was having none of this and pushed me off again into the flow. 'You can do it! Keep going! We'll be waiting for you in Central Park. Go!'

First Avenue is the stretch of the course that's supposed to lift your spirits, but it destroyed mine. It stretched on and on and on into the distance. There wasn't a single turn in the road. A 4-mile straight line of deafening noise, skyscrapers and bobbing heads as far as my eye could see. I seemed to be slowing down. I started to panic, imagining people at home tracking my progress and seeing I had almost ground to a halt. A fear of failure took hold. The running demons stepped in. There are two of them, one on each shoulder. I discovered their power that day and they have stayed with me ever since. Sometimes I don't hear them for miles during a race and then suddenly they appear. Other times they are arguing from the minute I cross the start line. This is how they go:

Good Demon: 'You're doing OK, feeling good, pacing well, perhaps a little too fast? Pull it back, rein it in a little? All that training is done. Think of this as a victory lap. Enjoy the crowds. Feed off their energy, the noise, all those faces. Look at them willing you on.'

Bam! Out of nowhere the Evil Demon pipes up: 'You're too old for this. Why on earth do you keep putting yourself through it? What are you trying to prove? You have done enough marathons now. It's hurting you. You want to stop, don't you? You want to stop and put your head in your hands and cry.'

Beep beep. That's my running watch telling me that I have just ticked off another mile.

Good Demon: 'You see! This is OK. You're on track. Your pace is still good. You're going faster than you thought. Listen to all those feet around you, thousands of them hitting the tarmac almost in sync. Metronomic. Count to 20. Distract yourself. Only 10 more miles to go. Visualise that. Think of the finish line, the medal at the end.'

Evil Demon: 'Hahaha. Ten more miles. That is such a long way. You are so tired. You can't keep this up that long. Watch your heart rate. It's rising. Remember what happened the first time you ran a marathon. Your heart started racing and then you collapsed. Slow down. Walk? Why don't you walk? There's a drinks station coming up.'

Good Demon: 'Don't walk. Do not walk. Do not stop. Just distract yourself. Get through this bit. Think of something else. It's so hard to start running again once you walk. Smile at the crowd. Think how lucky you are to be here. You are so lucky to be able to do this.'

By now, on First Avenue, I was walking. My mind was crumbling, exhausted by the mental battle going on between the demons. I told myself it didn't matter, this was just a bit of fun, I didn't care. I took a photo on my phone. Another runner, also walking, said, 'Hey, I'll take a photo of you if you want?' So, I actually stopped and stood on the side of the road, posing for a couple of shots as runners passed me. Then I called Susie. 'What's happening?! I've been tracking you. You've done 18 miles; you've not stopped, have you?' she shouted down the phone. I could hardly hear her, but I moaned and groaned and whinged about how tired I was, how I couldn't do this, how I was now walking, how I'd had enough. Susie knew me very well by now and she knew exactly how to handle my collapsing morale. 'Soph, Tim is less than a mile ahead of you. You're faster than him. I've been tracking him too and he's slowing down. Get on with it. Run. Go and catch him. At least you'll have someone to run with if you do.'

I caught Tim as I came off the Willis Avenue Bridge into the Bronx in the final few miles before Central Park. He was indeed struggling, in the pain cave, as he later said. Funnily enough I was feeling better by now.

I waved at him, but he didn't see me, so I moved on, my competitive spark fully alight now, though my hope of finishing in under 4 hours was disappearing fast. I spotted Richard again in the crowd and then threw myself at the finish line, stepping over it in an annoying 4 hours and 2 minutes. I kicked myself for wasting so much time out there on the course. My head had let me down more than my body. Still to this day I have never shown anyone that photo of me standing stock-still by the road in the middle of the marathon in my Union Jack running vest, posing, not running. But I have kept it as a reminder to never ever give up.

---

'Less than a parkrun to go,' I shout at Susie as we near the end of the Chicago 2017 Marathon. It's our usual race mantra that normally makes us both smile. Not this time. She is grimacing now. She has been coughing so violently in the last few days, filling herself with the strongest cough medicine she could find at the pharmacy, which has left her feeling woozy. We're almost at 24 miles. I'm surprised she has made it this far. *We can walk to the end if we have to,* I keep thinking. In the past year we have flown around the world together, ticking off the Berlin Marathon and then Tokyo. Chicago is the culmination of our three-and-a-half-year quest to get our Six Star Medals. We have to finish this race together.

Our race has been steady enough, a fairly good sub-4-hour pace. But once we hit 20 miles I could tell by the look on her face that Susie was really struggling. We have run so many miles together now since Boston that no words are needed. And it must be bad if she is slowing to an almost walk. Susie is the one who has driven me on and pushed me into new zones when I didn't think I had it in me. 'It's only 4 hours of your life,' she'll cajole me if I am fretting about a race. 'One foot in front of the other and we'll make it to the end.' She has a core of steel when it comes to pushing herself into extreme zones of discomfort, even pain. 'Let's get it done,' is her constant refrain as I hold on to her heels. Now, though, I'm having to wait for her by the roadside after getting ahead and it's discombobulating.

With a mile to go, we try to pick up the pace on a slight incline. I grab her hand as we see the finish line and run, arms in the air, under the gantry with just 2 minutes to spare before the clock hits 4 hours. Almost immediately, the coughing starts again. She really shouldn't have run. But we ignore this fact as we are ushered towards the blue Abbott World Marathon Majors area. One of the bosses of the London Marathon, Nick Bitel, is there and surprises us as he appears for our 'medal presentation'. A TV crew wants to interview us. Susie is looking more and more spaced out. The reporter starts asking us questions and I'm halfway through a reply when I turn to Susie and realise she's not standing next to me anymore. She has fainted and is now lying by my feet. She comes round quickly and I help her up, apologising to the reporter as I half drag, half carry her away in search of help.

The medical tent is a fascinating, often shocking place to be on marathon day. Unconscious runners being stretchered in, people on drips or throwing up. You see first-hand just how hard people are prepared to push themselves after months of training. Susie is propped up on a plastic chair, smiling again. We have somehow convinced the medical staff that I am Susie's next of kin. Now they want to put her on a drip. 'No way,' she keeps saying to me. Then there's a commotion as a woman who looks like she is unconscious is stretchered in, distracting the doctors. 'Come on, Soph. I'm not nearly that bad. Get me out of here. I'm not having a needle put in me.' So, I bust her out.

The walk back to the hotel is very slow and we are making a racket. Our gang all have two medals each now – the Chicago Marathon medal and the huge Six Star Medal that we first glimpsed in Boston more than three years ago. As we walk, they clank together, like cowbells. I am having to concentrate on Susie though, holding her upright as she grabs on to lamp posts to steady herself. Then suddenly, two blocks away from my hotel, she just stops and announces that she has to lie down on the pavement in the middle of Chicago. 'I'm all right,' she keeps saying, coughing, as pedestrians step over and around her. 'Just let me rest here for a moment. I'll be OK.' My hotel is nearer than hers, so we get her back there and put her into my bed with tea and a dressing gown, while the rest of us celebrate our Six Star Medals in the bar.

Ten days later, back in the UK, Susie goes to the doctor. There are tests, more tests and an X-ray and an ultrasound. It is months before her cough is properly diagnosed and the results are not good. There's a lump in her throat that is blocking her air tubes. She needs an operation to take it out. It is scheduled for February 2018, just eight weeks before Susie and I are due to fly off for the biggest challenge of my life. I have finally given in to her and signed up for the Marathon des Sables, the 150-mile multi-stage ultra over a week across the Sahara Desert, which she has already run three times now. 'Don't worry, Soph,' she says. 'We are going. I'm not letting you do that race without me. I will be there.' But given the diagnosis, I just cannot believe she will.

# 4

## *Preparing to go the extra mile*

There is a roaring sound in the black night. It is sudden and deafening, shocking. I am jolted awake. Our open-sided tent is flapping violently in the wind. My face is being stung by grains of sand whipped across the desert floor. Around me, the faint outlines of exhausted bodies moving now, their heads lifting towards the noise, disappearing quickly again into sleeping bags, taking cover from the sand. We have only been asleep for a couple of hours after a 24-mile run across the Sahara Desert. Eight of us are lying in a line in a Berber tent, a simple black awning propped up by three wooden poles, open to the elements on two sides. Our shelter is shaking, heaving.

Susie is here, lying next to me. She has made it to Morocco, finally recovered from her operation. Now one of the poles gives way and lands on her, narrowly missing her head. We had been warned about sandstorms and the power they hold. But it is the noise that astonishes me. I feel exposed and vulnerable, tiny in the swirl of nature's force. Head torches go on, small beams of light popping up across this vast camp of runners in the middle of the desert. There are more than a thousand of us here. But right now, we feel very alone. I can hardly open my eyes. There's too much sand in the air, in my mouth, in my sleeping bag. It is everywhere. I can hear the shouts and panic from runners who've forgotten to put away the clothes they had left drying in the daytime heat. Now they are up and chasing their belongings through camp as they spin off in the violent wind. Tired, stiff legs after two days of long runs jolted into action to try to stop vital kit being carried off in swirling sand. A sleeping mat cartwheels past us and disappears into the dark beyond. There's a shout from our tent as the sides rear up and one of our tentmates who was sleeping at the edge finds himself exposed to the full force of the storm. His only extra clothing layer for the night-time cold is sucked out. I watch it happening in slow motion. Up and down, up and down, the edge of the tent lifting with each gust of the wind. Tim's silhouette appears and disappears, jerking awkwardly like an old-fashioned cartoon. His one pair of running socks is gone, he shouts. His jacket too. You carry nothing surplus in this race. You need everything you have. How can he run on tomorrow, another 18 miles, if his socks are gone?

I'm lying next to the main wooden pole in the middle of the tent that holds the whole thing up. It is shaking and bending in the wind. So, I sit up and put my back to it, trying to keep it upright, as I'm buffeted around. I stay like that for at least half an hour, while the others attempt to hold the sides down. As the storm howls on, my fear starts to ease. We may be in the middle of the desert, but nothing, except this tent, will land on us, I tell myself. We can't be hurt, not badly at least. Our tent is on the edge of camp, the outer circle. The storm is blowing from behind us, right through the heart of camp. Some tents are now collapsing on top of their occupants. I have stuffed all my belongings into the bottom of my sleeping bag. The sand in my teeth crunches every time I try to speak.

In our tent everyone reacts differently. Shaun, ex-Army, who has spent months living in ditches in Iraq and Afghanistan, barely moves. He seems to sleep through the whole thing. Susie, a three-time veteran of this race, has seen it all before. 'I told you not to leave stuff lying around in the tent,' she shouts at me, as she pops her head out of her sleeping bag for a moment. 'Listen to all those people out there chasing after their belongings that weren't pinned down.' Nick, the vet from Hong Kong, whose wife has calculated, cooked, boxed up and labelled all his food for the week (our daily surprise is to find out what he's got) is next to me. He is by far the most worried of the lot, determined to cling on to the one pole that is still just about holding our bivouac up. But after an hour or so, we give up. We need to sleep before the morning's long run across Moroccan mountains to the next camp and this storm is not letting up.

Susie shuffles across, closer to her husband, Shaun, making space for Tim in the middle of the tent. He is the only one with an inflatable mattress. Mine burst on day one. Since then, I've been sleeping with just the tent floor between me and the stony ground. I feel a wave of envy and prop my knee on the very edge of the soft mattress. It's a shred of comfort. And then we let the last pole standing fall, bringing the heavy tent down on our heads. We are completely entombed. The fabric comes to rest just centimetres from our faces. Buried in a bivouac.

The wind howls around us. The sand piles up outside. I imagine that I am at home, cocooned under my duvet, warm, safe. Finally, exhausted, we all fall asleep.

---

I had landed myself here in the desert thanks to a drunken Christmas party 18 months earlier. I was 48 and really struggling with the idea of getting older. A friend, who was also about to hit 50, had already run the Marathon des Sables, or MDS as it's known, and had been thinking about going back again for the challenge. Somehow over dinner and far too much wine, we talked ourselves into signing up. When I told Susie, she was outraged. 'That's my race!' she declared. 'You're not going without me!' So, she signed up too, and so did Shaun and Tim. And then more friends joined us. Suddenly there were six of us going. It was a very expensive race to enter – £4200 in total, which included a return flight to Morocco, two nights at a hotel once I finished the race and the cost of repatriation in case I died. It has happened. All my friends paid up, so I had to follow. Suddenly there was no turning back.

The MDS is a legendary race that was started by a Frenchman called Patrick Bauer. He had been living in West Africa in the 1980s, selling encyclopaedias to teachers and books on medicine to doctors and pharmacists. He crossed the Sahara many times by car. But he decided he wanted to do it on foot and alone. So, in 1984 he set off on a 12-day journey covering more than 200 miles. He didn't see another human being in that time. His backpack weighed 35kg because he had to carry all his water as well as food. When he returned to France and began telling people about his adventure, runners he knew started saying they wanted to have a go too. He launched his first Marathon des Sables in 1986. Twenty-four runners took part that year – all of them French except for one Moroccan. By the time I made it to the start line over 30 years later, more than a thousand people were lining up with me from all over the world.

It is billed as the toughest footrace on earth, though the truth is it's not. There are much harder races out there, but this one comes with its own unique challenges. And there is something magical about it. It is six marathons in five days, 150 miles (more than 250 kilometres) across Saharan sands, carrying everything you will need to survive for a week on your back – all your food, a stove to boil water, a sleeping bag, the compulsory medical kit, a compass, even a venom pump in case you tread on a scorpion or snake. All you are given is a Berber tent to sleep under at night, a rationed amount of water every day and brown plastic poo bags to be used in the makeshift toilet tents around camp. There is no running water.

When I signed up and paid my deposit in December 2016, the race felt a long way off. I told myself I had 18 months to drop out if I couldn't do it. I needed to have an escape option. I had never run more than 26.2 miles before. I was going to have to run a lot further than that. On the fourth day of the MDS, you have to complete an ultramarathon – around 56 miles in one go. And that would be after three days of running pretty much three marathons in a row. I had no idea if I could run an ultramarathon. So, I signed up for my first one, knowing that if I couldn't manage that, there was no way I would be able to take on the Sahara. Susie came with me. After years of telling me that ultras were 'great fun' – you get to walk and eat cake, she'd always say, laughing – she couldn't leave me on my own. The race we chose was the North Downs Way 50. It helped that it started almost at her front door in Farnham, Surrey. Ahead of us lay 50 miles along the hilly National Trail that loosely follows the ancient Pilgrims' Way to Canterbury. I had run the London Marathon a month before, so I was 'marathon fit', but I had done no extra training for this. I had told almost no one that I was doing it. That way, when I failed, I could fail quietly. The distance loomed large in my head. Fifty miles. *Like running from London to Oxford*, I kept thinking. I could picture that journey in a car. I couldn't imagine how I was going to be able to do that on foot within the 13-hour time limit allowed.

We gathered in a village hall just after 6 a.m. on a May Saturday morning in 2017. There was a kit check at registration to make sure we had a survival blanket, a waterproof jacket, a whistle to attract help if needed, a head torch and a GPS tracker. We set off for the start at the North Downs Way trail head, walking along a busy dual carriageway in Farnham to get there. But as soon as we stepped on to the trail, we were plunged into car-free countryside that would continue for 50 miles to Kent.

Ultra running happens at a different pace, a slower pace, one that you can keep going at over the miles and miles ahead. It felt strange shuffling slowly off with hundreds of other trail runners after years of road racing on tarmac against the clock. The first 10 miles were a relatively gentle ramble along sandy paths, across fields and through villages towards Guildford. Then the hills began. 'If you can roll a marble down it, then we're walking up it,' declared Susie, though it was more of a march. With more than 5500 feet (that's almost 1700m) of climbing ahead, we had to keep our legs as fresh as we could.

There were checkpoints along the way, every 6 miles or so, run by cheerful volunteers who helped us refill water bottles and thrust copious amounts of sugar-filled treats our way. I relished the pause, a chance to catch my breath and rest. But Susie started hustling me through each one, watching the clock. 'We're wasting time here! Let's get this done,' she kept saying. At the top of Box Hill, we cheered and laughed as I broke through 27 miles for the first time, the furthest I had ever run in one go. And yet we were only just over halfway through this race, with plenty more energy-sapping steep climbs ahead. We marched up hill after hill.

As we passed through 40 miles, the muscles in my thighs burnt on a steep downhill run. I winced with each step before being thrown into an eye-poppingly steep climb that left us both clutching our thighs, laughing and groaning in pain. My legs were stiffening up. My trail shoes were heavy with mud. My exhausted mind was longing for a finish line. We ticked through 50 miles, turned on to tarmac at last, heard a loudspeaker, glimpsed a blue inflatable finish line in a field and ran for it with every last ounce of energy in us. We had done it: 51.3 miles in 10 hours, 33 minutes. I was officially an ultra runner. 'You should try the 100-miler next,' someone shouted at me, just after I crossed the line. I laughed and shook my head. 'You see!' said Susie, smiling and nudging me. 'You CAN do it. I told you that you could. You will be absolutely fine in Morocco.' My desert exit strategy wasn't going well.

I became increasingly dependent on Susie. We had only known each other for three years but in that time the limits to which we had pushed ourselves in races together had already brought a deep level of trust. She had seen me at my most vulnerable, most knackered, most exposed, in a way that friends who I'd known for decades hadn't. 'I refuse to run across the desert on my own,' I told her over and over again. 'You won't!' she kept saying. 'We will start and finish and go through every checkpoint together.'

Training for the Sahara was supposed to begin in October, as soon as we had recovered from the Chicago Marathon. Susie had been to her GP when we got back, to try to get rid of her hacking cough. Whooping cough is what was initially diagnosed and she was given a flu jab. But the coughing continued. Three weeks later she texted me. 'I found a lump in my neck yesterday and woke up worrying about it. I googled it – NEVER GOOGLE "LUMP". Should I go to a doctor?'

She went for an ultrasound. It revealed a 3-cm lump. 'Fuck,' texted Susie. 'They said it's probably fine, but I need to get it checked. I didn't really know what to say and instantly forgot everything the doctor told me. I'm sure it's OK. I have far too much to do in the next few months anyway. We have a desert race to run.'

We were supposed to be running another ultramarathon that week in Wendover Woods in Hertfordshire as part of our training, another 50 miles of huge climbs, a lot of it in the dark this time. Susie pulled out. She was struggling to sleep at night with a constant feeling that something was pushing on her windpipe. I pulled out too. I wasn't running an ultra without her.

The next few weeks became a confusing world of training, desert race kit planning, booking sessions in a heat chamber in Kingston and Susie's increasingly numerous medical appointments and then finally a diagnosis.

'Turns out I have a large tumour growing in my neck,' she texted. 'After what can only be described as a stressful week with visits to a consultant, a specialist and a biopsy, (two bottles of gin, three bottles of wine and a good dose of sleeping pills), results are back and it's "probably benign". The other news is as it's large – 4cm – and squashing my windpipe, it needs to come out along with my thyroid. Thyroids regulate cake consumption. So, I need to get that figured out. BUT importantly, post op I'll be back running after two weeks.'

It was a lot to take in. But then nothing happened. No date for an operation was set. Susie went into full-on denial and didn't ask any more questions. 'They're pretty sure it's benign,' she kept saying. 'If they were worried, I would have heard from them.'

So, we ploughed on. By Christmas we were running at least 50 miles a week with back-to-back runs – 15 miles one day, then 10 miles the next day, to get used to running on tired legs. We planned long runs every weekend with Shaun and Tim. Point-to-point 20-milers or more along the Thames Path, through Windsor Great Park or in the Surrey Hills. I'd wear the rucksack I had bought for the desert, getting used to the weight I would have to carry by loading it up with tins of baked beans, boxes of washing powder, anything that I could find in the cupboard at home to weigh myself down as I jangled along slowly. Our peak training would be in February when I'd have to run about 70 miles in one week before 'tapering down', allowing my body to recover before we headed to the desert in April.

It was a struggle to fit it all in around work but I started running to Broadcasting House in Oxford Circus, a 10k run from home to the newsroom. I would run home again if I needed to. One of my legs started playing up. 'I'm having a massive confidence crisis,' I texted Susie. 'I just don't think I'll be able to do the Marathon des Sables. My leg is so sore. It hurts to run on it.' This in hindsight seems a strange thing to have been texting my friend who had a lump in her neck. I think we were both in denial. 'REST and STOP WORRYING,' she typed back. 'You will be FINE.'

Our last big run was another ultramarathon called the Pilgrim Challenge. The race was 66 miles along the North Downs Way again, but this time it was over two days. Thirty-three miles out, sleep on the floor of a school or pay for a room at the local Travelodge in Redhill, then 33 miles back the next day, in February, when the weather was likely to be difficult and the trail deep in mud. 'If you can do this, you'll be absolutely fine in the desert,' said Susie, who was running it with me, along with Shaun and Tim, our desert gang.

Then out of the blue I had another text from Susie two weeks before the race: 'The lump in my neck is bigger. It's across the front of my neck now. I can see it. Going to try to see the GP.'

The GP sent her to a consultant. The consultant called her in for tests. I went to the hospital with her 'to take notes' and ask questions for her. 'I can't take it all in,' she kept saying.

The operation was scheduled for 2 February, the day before Pilgrims. The lump on her thyroid was even bigger now. The test results were inconclusive. 'Probably benign,' they said again, 'but we do need to get it out now. Then we'll know.' Susie and Shaun would obviously not be running the ultra. Tim called me. 'We're going to have to do it on our own,' I said nervously. 'I feel like a kid off on a big adventure without my parents. I hope we can get through it.'

I now had to contemplate the reality that Susie and Shaun may not make it to the desert at all. On top of that, I felt increasingly guilty about going when I had young kids at home. Our nanny, Mimi, who'd worked for us for 14 years, suddenly quit. 'I can't watch you go off into the desert like this. You might die,' she said to me in front of Richard, which was not exactly helpful. Two days later, she changed her mind and said she was staying, presumably in case I did.

The lump that came out of Susie's neck was even bigger than expected: 7cm long, a dark red solid mass that looked like an exotic reddish plum. I know this because she sent me a photo of it laid out on the surgeon's table 'to cheer me up' while I was running on day one of the Pilgrims race. I opened the message just after Tim and I had crossed the finish line at the school near Redhill. I couldn't believe she had had that in her throat.

The first stage of this ultra, 33 miles of muddy trails, hadn't been as bad as I'd feared. Tim and I ran together at a steady pace along a path we both now knew well. Many of the other runners were also signed up for the desert and it was reassuring to find I could keep up with them. Some were running with their fully weighted MDS backpacks on, around 10kg, which is what I'd have to do too but I was worried about getting injured so kept mine lighter for this race.

I felt a little guilty as we jumped in a taxi at the end of day one, leaving behind dozens of people who had chosen to sleep on the floor in a school's gymnasium. They were testing out their MDS sleeping mats and kit, opening their packets of dried expedition food that we'd have to survive on for a week in Morocco. I decided that could wait until I was actually in the desert and could do nothing about it. Tim and I had chosen the Travelodge and the all-you-can-eat buffet – huge plates of Yorkshire pudding, beef, cauliflower and gravy topped off with enormous ice-cream sundaes.

My legs were so stiff when I woke up the next morning. *How can I possibly run another 33 miles back to Farnham?* I kept thinking. We lined up again at the school near Redhill and waited to start. The first mile or so back was uphill and it hurt. But 4 miles in and we were high up on flat ground, blue sky, big views across the Surrey countryside and I was amazed how normal my legs were starting to feel. There's something psychologically easier about an out-and-back race. We were heading home. I felt OK now. I knew I would get this done. Tim fell behind with about 15 miles to go and waved me on. I was feeling strong. So, I kept going, ticking off the miles and thinking of the field with the finishing tent, my medal, and knowing that Susie, who was out of hospital already, would be tracking my every step online. 'Just a parkrun to go,' I shouted out to myself with 3 miles left.

The relief was enormous when I saw the finish line. I was eighth woman overall and couldn't stop grinning. 'You SUPERSTAR,' texted Susie. 'I'm so sorry I wasn't there to cheer you over the line. I wanted to be but just couldn't.'

Tim and I drove over to her house on the way home from the race. It was only a couple of miles away. My legs were so rigid by now that I couldn't dodge her massive British bulldog, Roy, when he threw himself at me, almost knocking me over. Susie looked terrible, puffy and sore, eating small bits of ice cream to try to get the swelling in her throat down. She could barely walk.

A week later, she was back in hospital again. This desert adventure was looking more and more unlikely. Her throat had swollen up and she had a fever. They whisked her straight into the operating theatre to open her up again and drain what was now a major infection. A week later the test results on the lump came back.

'It was cancer. Shitting hell,' she typed to me at dawn one morning. 'I'm sitting here – everyone is asleep – googling thyroid cancer. Going to stop googling now. It's frightening me. It was big though. The cancer bit was almost 2cm. It grew very quickly.'

Encapsulated papillary thyroid carcinoma was what they told her she had. 'Encapsulated sounds good?' I typed back. 'That means contained, hasn't spread, doesn't it?' She sent me the histology report, which neither of us could understand. I sent it straight on to one of my best friends, a doctor, who looked at it for her. 'Looks OK actually as far as any cancer goes!' said my friend Caty. 'Tell her I wouldn't start making a bucket list quite yet . . . 95 per cent survival rate, which is pretty much the same as you and me.'

Susie's doctors confirmed that the cancer had been contained and hadn't spread. They had got it all out. She didn't need any more treatment at all. She had been very lucky.

Two weeks later we were both on the start line of a race called the Big Half, by London's Tower Bridge. 'This seems completely nuts,' I said to her. 'You've only just had an operation! Did the doctors say you could run a half marathon this soon?' 'Yes,' she said, and then ducked down to check her shoelaces. 'Actually . . . that's a lie. I didn't ask them. So at least I am not disobeying orders...'

I understood her need to run again. We trained so hard and ran so much now that we felt incredibly fit, invincible. Cancer at the age of 42 was a curveball that she still couldn't understand. Her body had let her down. Now she was determined to put the last few months behind her and get back out there again. And in four weeks' time we were heading to the Sahara.

---

Preparing for the Marathon des Sables involves intricate planning: scales, spreadsheets, calorie counting. I was going to have to carry everything I needed for six days in my backpack, including all my food. Susie had drawn up long lists of what I would need – a small, light camping stove and fuel bricks to heat water for my freeze-dried food, a venom pump, an emergency kit, a desert hat, water bottles, cutlery, a penknife, a head torch, a sleeping bag that would be warm enough for the sub-zero nights in the desert. And I was going to have to run carrying all of it. The shoes I chose could make or break the race. My feet would swell in the heat and so I was told to wear shoes that were half a size bigger. I needed desert gaiters too to stop the sand getting in and rubbing my feet raw. The gaiters were pieces of nylon elasticated just under my knees and attached with Velcro around the side of each shoe. 'I almost forgot. Buy some paw wax,' Susie texted out of the blue. 'You need it to toughen your feet before we go.' Paw wax? I looked it up. It was for dogs to stop their paws getting cracked. I called her in disbelief. 'You want me to put dogs' paw treatment on my feet?!' 'Yes, I do,' she replied. 'Or you could bathe them in methylated spirits instead?' I ignored both suggestions.

Most of the weight I would be carrying would be from my food. We would have to provide enough for ourselves for six whole days plus breakfast on the seventh day before a 'charity walk' out of the desert. The rules said everyone had to carry a minimum of 2000 calories a day. That's not a lot when you're doing extreme exercise in extreme heat. I pored over a spreadsheet drawn up by a friend, Emily, who had done the race with Susie a few years before. One thousand calories in freeze-dried porridge for breakfast, high-calorie cashews, salami, lumps of Parmesan (vacuum-packed) and energy gels for lunch, another thousand calories for dinner with a packet of freeze-dried macaroni cheese or Thai green curry, all brought to edible life by hot water from my stove. I decided to take 3000 calories a day in total to keep me going and parcelled it all up into daily rations to ensure I didn't run out.

As the race got closer, the pressure became intense. I banned Susie from mentioning me in any of her numerous social media posts about her training. I made her crop me out of all of her photos. No one was to know I was going with her. She found keeping it quiet excruciatingly difficult. But she did as I asked. I remained invisible. 'Are you excited yet?' she kept texting as the race got closer. I wasn't. I was consumed by fear. At night I dreamt of getting lost in the desert, of dying, of leaving my three young children without a mother. I asked myself over and over again why I was doing this, why I was putting myself in so much danger. I was the woman who had collapsed at the London Marathon seven years earlier because I had overheated in temperatures of 20°C. Now I was about to head into the Sahara to run in hot sand dunes, under the burning sun in a hostile environment where the thermometer would likely top 50°C. What on earth was I doing?

Susie had booked sessions for her, Shaun and me in the heat chamber at Kingston University for the fortnight running up to our departure. I went there every morning before work, arriving at 6.30 a.m. It was a box with a treadmill and exercise bike inside and a glass window by the sealed door so that Dr Chris Howe could keep an eye on us as he raised the temperature up to desert heat levels. We spent an hour in there each time with our heavy backpacks on, alternating between the bike and jogging slowly on the treadmill. Dr Howe took our temperature before we entered the chamber and then monitored us as our core body temperature rose. The heat was horrendous but it was made worse by the humidity. The more we sweated, the more humid it got. And Shaun in particular sweated a lot. It poured off him in torrents. With three of us in there it soon felt like being in the tropics. I could not imagine running in this day after day. An hour was bad enough.

I started to panic. 'Don't be freaked out,' Susie said, trying to reassure me. 'The heat in the desert is much drier than this. It won't feel this bad. And there'll be doctors everywhere. It's hot for sure, but I have never felt as bad out there as I do in the heat chamber. And don't forget you've got another whole week of heat training to go. You are going to be stronger, much stronger than you think.'

A week before we left Susie arrived on my doorstep with scales. All my food and kit were laid out on the bedroom floor. 'We can trim this stuff down,' she said. I couldn't imagine how. My backpack weighed 7.4kg − without water. What was she going to make me leave behind? Not food? She was brutal. We weighed everything. My spare pair of shorts and the tiniest vest to change into after we ran each day. Even the loo roll I had packed, all 58g of it. 'Take the cardboard tube out of the middle,' she ordered. I was made to cut the handle off my toothbrush and take the plastic case off my compass. I was taking lightweight collapsible running poles. 'Do you really need them?' she asked. She wasn't taking any. My inflatable pillow and my flip-flops were deemed unnecessary luxury items. 'But this pillow is so small! What am I going to sleep on?' I moaned.

'And my flip-flops? They don't weigh much. And I'll want to take my trainers off, won't I?' 'I use my trainers as my pillow,' said Susie, 'and you don't need flip-flops. We won't be doing much walking once we are back in the tent every day!' I ignored her. The pillow and flip-flops were coming with me.

A week before we were leaving, a letter landed on our front door mat. It was from the Marathon des Sables team, on headed notepaper.

*30/03/18*

*The MDS Team*
*Dear Sophie Raworth,*

*We are very sorry to inform you that we have just heard that a sandstorm is due to hit the Sahara Desert from next Thursday onwards. Therefore, the team organisers and insurers have confirmed that we can no longer go ahead with the 2018 Marathon des Sables.*

*We know you have done a lot of training, but the good news is you will be able to spend the week in Portugal with your family, who were going to miss you very much.*

*Sincerely,*
*The MDS Team*

'April Fools,' shouted my children, as they burst out into the hallway laughing. I was taken aback by just how relieved I had momentarily felt, a huge weight fleetingly lifted off my shoulders.

My final hope of an exit was my husband. The day before my flight to Morocco, I told him that I was worried about going in case something happened to me and that taking such risks with three young children at home was irresponsible. On top of that our nanny Mimi, who'd resigned to try to stop me going to the desert and then unresigned two days later, had announced that she now felt so 'inspired' by my desert adventure that she was off to trek the Great Wall of China. She had already gone. My husband, now without a nanny or wife for two weeks, stopped and stared at me. For a moment I thought he was about to agree that this was all a ridiculous idea and thank me for finally coming to my senses. Instead, he laughed out loud. 'You have done all the training,' he said. 'You have been preparing for this for MONTHS. Of course you are going to do it. The kids and I are taking you to the airport in the morning.'

# 5

## *Feeling the fear and doing it anyway*

We step off the plane and out into a blast of dry heat at Ouarzazate Airport in southern Morocco. It's a sharp contrast to the April dampness and grey skies we left behind at Gatwick. We'd flown in on a specially chartered flight for the 363 British runners heading into the desert, most of whom were men. I'd sat a row behind Susie and Shaun, in among people I didn't know. My family had just waved me off at Gatwick. My youngest child, Ollie, who was 10, was far more focused on the week he was about to have with his sisters and dad on a beach in Portugal than on where his mother was going. I'd mentioned my children a couple of times to the men sitting around me on the plane, testing the waters to see how shocked they would be that I had young kids and had just left them behind. 'My wife is at home with our two-year-old,' said one man next to me. 'My wife is pregnant with our third child. She's gone off to stay with her parents,' said another. Most of these men had kids too, much younger than mine. They seemed completely unfazed by leaving them. I needed to calm down.

The airport at Ouarzazate is small, a caramel-coloured building with a few palm trees and flags, the only other colour in this dusty, rugged landscape. The terminal fills quickly with runners, all of us clutching our MDS backpacks. We've got this far. We can't lose our vital kit now. As we walk out of Arrivals into the sunshine, dozens of race organisers and staff, all dressed in the same dark brown gilets and khaki shorts, are lined up on either side of the path, clapping and cheering as we drag our luggage behind us. It's strange to be applauded when all we have done is arrive. In the middle of the throng is Patrick Bauer, the Frenchman who started this race 32 years ago, godlike, a star attraction with a confident swagger, kissing people on both cheeks. He is enjoying the attention. I stick limpet-like to Susie as we are ushered on to one of the fleet of coaches lined up in front of Arrivals.

Ouarzazate is the gateway to the Sahara, the door to the desert, though we still have a six-hour drive south to go. Our coach is full of nervous energy. I sit next to Susie, listening to the chatter around us, people talking about the training they've done, the other races they've run. One of the race organisers walks along the aisle, giving out a small booklet. Hands reach out to grab one. 'It's the Roadbook,' says Susie. 'They keep the route secret and they change it every year. We are about to find out what is in store for us. I just hope they haven't made the longest run too horrible.' She grabs her copy and flicks straight to Day four, the long stage: 53 miles, all in one go. The map is a black-and-white sketch of the route weaving over dried riverbeds, mountains and what look like rather a lot of sand dunes. 'That's not too bad,' she says. 'One year we had to do more than 60 miles.' I open my copy and try to take it all in.

'Well done, you made it,' it says on page one. 'This bus is transporting you to a slightly mad adventure that's bound to be wonderful. In two days' time, on April 8th, surrounded by 1100 course companions, you'll be setting off to the sound of AC/DC's "Highway to Hell" to live out your destiny: seven days of running, dozens and dozens of kilometres of desert from which you won't emerge the same.'

I turn the pages slowly, trying to decipher what we will be doing. The distances, now that I see them in black and white, seem enormous:

Day one – 30.3km (18.8 miles)
Day two – 39km (24.2 miles)
Day three – 31.6km (19.6 miles)
Day four – 86.2km (53.6 miles)
Day five – rest day (if you have already finished the 86.2km/53.6 miles)
Day six – 42.2km (26.2 miles) and the end of the race
Day seven – a 7.7km (4.8 miles) 'charity walk' out of the desert

I don't speak very much during the long drive south. We're heading close to the border with Algeria, which is where our first camp, or bivouac as it's called, has been set up. I spend a lot of the journey gazing out of the window, taking in the mountainous, arid landscape that stretches out all around us, valleys, steep climbs, with only our snaking coach convoy visible on the twisting roads. We pass through small towns with their ochre-coloured buildings two or three storeys high. Almost all of them have unfinished top floors. People stare up at us as we drive through, fascinated by these strange tourists peering back out. Small patches of green spring up, visible from afar, palm trees, life, water, an oasis. Signs point along dusty roads to hotels or restaurants. I wonder how many people ever turn off and stop there. The further we travel, the fewer people we see. We are going off-grid.

I call Richard in search of normality. When he answers, I can hear our children laughing in the background. They've just arrived in Portugal. Rather a lot of me is starting to wish I were there too. 'I have never felt so out of my comfort zone,' I whisper into the phone. 'I really don't know if I can do this.' 'You'll be fine,' he tells me. 'Don't worry. You've got Susie and Shaun there. They'll look after you. Stay together.'

A few hours into the journey and the coach convoy pulls over on the roadside in the middle of nowhere. It's 4 p.m. and we still have a long way to go. This is a late lunch stop and we file off the coach into a rocky scrubland, like schoolchildren, clutching paper bags full of sandwiches and huge fresh oranges that have been handed out. Perched on rocks by the roadside, we sit in a line looking out at a mountain range and eat. People disappear into gullies in search of quiet places to go to the loo. There's very little to hide behind. It's strange to think we won't see a proper toilet or running water for more than a week now.

It is getting dark by the time we arrive at the bivouac. We pour out of the coaches, dragging our suitcases awkwardly across the sand, a ragtag bunch of adventure-seekers in the midlife crisis zone – the average age is 50, I'm told. That's a milestone I'll be hitting in just four weeks' time. There are people here from all walks of life, quite a lot of them are Army or ex-Army and City types. There are only 175 women in the whole race.

The camp is vast. It is made up of three incomplete circles of black tents. A woman wearing a head torch and sitting at a wobbly plastic table checks us all in and assigns us a tent for the race. We are given tent 128 on the outer ring, the British zone. It'll be home to eight of us for the whole week.

The tents are the kind used by nomadic Berbers – a few wooden poles with a black goat's hair canvas thrown over the top. Imagine a pitched roof on a house, sloping down on both sides and held up by poles in the middle. You have to duck down to get in. The front and back of the tent are open to the elements, allowing the air to blow through freely while keeping the scorching sun out. The floor is a dark green and beige swirling carpet, where we spread ourselves out. There's no room for our suitcases, which already look out of place. So we line them up along one of the tent's open sides, a windbreak for now. They'll be taken from us tomorrow and driven back to a hotel near the airport where we will end up in 10 days' time. If we make it, that is. I had imagined I'd be sleeping on soft Saharan sands, so I am surprised when I sit down on sharp stones. Susie gets us all to lift up the carpet so we can pick out the sharpest rocks as well as small circular thorn heads dotted all over the ground. 'Whoever finishes first every day – this is going to be your main task,' she announces. 'Get the stones, rocks and thorns out so the rest of us can just collapse when we get back here.' This is one job I know I won't be doing. I will never run fast enough to be the first back.

It's cold, too. Much colder than I'd imagined the desert to be at night. I am already so glad that I've brought a down jacket and didn't opt for the lighter hazmat-style suits that Susie and Shaun will be wearing all week. They look like forensic detectives. We have two nights here at this camp before the race starts. We have all brought cheap inflatable camping mattresses to sleep on for those first two nights. At least we will be well rested before the race starts. The mattresses are too big and heavy to carry so instead we will leave them with the teams of Berbers who move our tents every day. They'll be delighted to have them. I climb into my sleeping bag with proper pyjamas on for one last night. They'll be packed away tomorrow too, along with my portable phone charger, clean clothes, even my underwear. I don't want to carry a gram more on my back than I need to. From tomorrow I'll be wearing the same kit every day until we get to the end.

For the first time I see the stars. The most incredible canopy of galaxies, the Milky Way, thousands of pinpricks of light stretching out in every direction across the vast black sky. With no electricity out here for miles around, there is a depth to the space above us that I have never witnessed before. It is immense. Huge. Humbling. I feel very small. I lie on my back with my sleeping bag tight around me and stare at the sky as I fall asleep.

Dawn is purple first, then apricot and finally golden as the sun rises up through the tents across camp. Silhouetted bodies start moving around. There's no hurry. The race doesn't start until tomorrow. Food is provided for us today. Our last meal will be tonight. After that we have to fend for ourselves. Around me whispers and quiet chatter, then the laughter starts. I lie on my stomach watching, cocooned against the cold, and feel for the first time strangely calm. I will start this race. Who knows how many days I will last? But now that I'm here, the terrible fear of the unknown that has plagued me for months is beginning to disappear.

The loos are just beyond the outer ring of camp. White tarpaulin rectangles about 6 feet high are dotted around the perimeter. They're tethered down by ropes. Each block has three cubicles inside. There's a small queue by the one nearest us. Some people decide not to wait and walk on. The men turn their backs, wee and return to camp. It's easy for them. The few women I see walk much further off into the desert before squatting down. 'That's Day One behaviour,' says Susie, grinning. She has just woken up next to me. 'You wait. Give it a day or two and we'll all be so exhausted we'll be weeing right here next to the tent.'

I join the queue, still in my pyjamas, and when it's my turn I push open the tarpaulin flap. Inside is a green plastic four-legged stool with the middle cut out. There's no roof in here, just blue sky above me. I can hear a man in the next cubicle. He's unnervingly close. If I prodded the tarpaulin wall I could touch him. We have all been given biodegradable brown plastic poo bags. The idea is to stretch one over the sides of the stool and put a stone in the bottom of the bag to prevent any unfortunate gusts of wind blowing the contents back up. And then you sit down, do what you need to do, use your own loo paper, take the bag off, tie a knot in it and put it in a big bin nearby. It sounds horrendous. But once I have mastered it, I find it remarkably simple and clean, too. My one obsession is making sure that I am not in a cubicle at the same time as anyone else I know. Far too intimate.

Today is kit check day, admin day. It is also the day I say farewell to my suitcase. I pack everything up that I cannot take with me: pyjamas, an extra pair of shoes, my hairbrush and my book. There's a long pretty summer dress folded up in my bag that my eyes rest on briefly. I packed it for the two-day stay at the hotel back at Ouarzazate after the race. There's a dinner and a party. Will I get to wear it? Will I make it? Once packed, I drag my suitcase back through the sand and leave it by the luggage truck. I glance over my shoulder as I walk away. The last remnants of my normal life disappear behind me.

This is what I am left with. On my head is a white desert hat, with a flap of fabric down the back to keep the sun off my neck. White-rimmed sunglasses, with orange lenses, protect my eyes from the glare. I'm wearing a grey tight-fitted T-shirt and a grey 'skort', like a tennis skirt with yellow shorts peeking out from under it. On my feet, my blue Brooks Adrenaline road shoes, though you can't see their colour because they are completely covered by the white gaiters that make me look like I'm wearing carrier bags on my feet. Below my knees are calf guards, tight compression sleeves to try to support my muscles and tendons over the 150 or so miles ahead. On one wrist is my running watch, for now fully charged up, though I have no way of replenishing it so I can only hope it will last. On the other wrist is a yellow buff, wrapped around a few times, which will be used to mop up sweat during the day, protect from cold at night and to cover my face if a sandstorm whips up. The all-important backpack is full now of every possession

I have out here. Strapped to the sides are a rolled-up sleeping bag in an orange cover and a rolled-up self-inflating sleeping mat. On my front are two big water bottles with drinking tubes so I can sip without stopping and an extra yellow pouch across my stomach with plasters, salt tablets, energy gels and snacks – the things I will want to reach easily during the race. A month away from my 50th birthday, have I ever lived with so little?

Susie and I queue in hot sunshine to have our kit checked and get our race numbers. The rules for the Marathon des Sables are strict. The compulsory kit list is long, and the race team make sure that we have it all. Our food is inspected to make sure we have the minimum 2000 calories a day. An SOS button and a GPS tracker are attached to our backpacks to make sure the race team can find us if we get in trouble. They also attach a plastic tag that has numbers on it. At every checkpoint during the race, they will punch holes in it to track how many bottles of rationed water we are taking. The rules say backpacks must weigh at least 6.5kg and no more than 15kg without water. I pass the test. Mine is 9kg though that's heavier than I was expecting. It will be well over 10kg once I have filled up my water bottles. Susie has managed to weigh in at 7.5kg. I know what she's thinking. Those flip-flops, that pillow, those running poles. Though she doesn't say it. I've not trained with anything like this weight on my back. It will get lighter as I eat my way through the food. I'll just have to hope I can cope with it for the first day or two.

On the way back to our tent, we see camels for the first time, two of them, with their drivers crouching in the shade of a small scrubby tree. These are the camels you do not want to see during the Marathon des Sables. Each race stage has a cut-off, a maximum time that you are allowed to be out for on the course every day. The cut-offs are generous. The first stage, for example, is almost 19 miles and we are given 10 hours to complete it. Some people walk the entire race, which is harder than it sounds because they are on their feet for so much longer in the intense, searing heat, when the runners are already back in camp recovering for the next day. The camels bring up the rear, walking across the desert at the cut-off pace. If they catch up with you, you are disqualified from the race.

A small sandstorm blows through camp that evening. Swirling dust that makes us filthy before we've even begun. We take shelter in the big tent where our last dinner is laid out. A buffet of bread, pasta and a few salads. We eat as much as we can. By 9 p.m. we are all back in our tent. Lined up like gorged caterpillars, we fall asleep.

# 6

## *Going all in on the Highway to Hell*

**Day one**
**30.3km (18.8 miles)**
**222m (728 feet) of climbing**

The camp starts stirring at 6 a.m. Small flames flickering in stoves, runners milling about eating their breakfast, queuing for the loos, eyeing the time, which seems to disappear quickly. We have three hours until we start. I pull my small stove out of my backpack and pop my first fuel brick inside. I've only practised this once in my back garden in London. Now that I'm having to do it for real, I'm finding it a little harder. 'You forgot your piece of foil,' says Susie, who's doing the same next to me. 'Wrap it round the bottom to keep the wind out. That'll make it easier to light.' The flame takes hold. I sit cross-legged on the mat, pour water into my tin cooking pot, rummage around in my backpack for a tea bag and then wait for the water to boil. Breakfast will be a packet of freeze-dried porridge with blueberries containing 1000 calories brought to life by the hot water.

There are shouts as lorries draw up nearby. Teams of Berbers jump out and set to work removing the tents, which will be taken to our next camp almost 19 miles away. They don't wait for us to go: three of them just lift our tent up and over our heads, leaving us sitting on a carpet in the desert. There are dozens of people around me now, all sitting on carpets. It's such a strange sight. I offer one of the Berbers my big inflatable mattress, which I can't carry with me. He nods and takes it with a smile, piling it on top of all the others. I wonder where they will end up in this desert.

Susie is studying today's route in our Roadbook. 'It doesn't look too bad today, Soph. Dried riverbeds, a lot of hard, stony ground and not too many sand dunes, so that'll be easier on the legs.' I listen and don't say much. I need to get my backpack ready. I pack, unpack, repack, unpack again. There's so much to squeeze in. 'Come on! Enough kit faffing,' says one of my tentmates, laughing. They're all waiting for me now.

The start line is on the edge of camp, a giant inflatable white arch. Runners are streaming towards it. Helicopters hover overhead. I can see the cameramen leaning out. We move into the middle of the throng. I don't let Susie out of my sight. The elites head to the front. Wiry, tall Moroccans who dominate this race every year, the El Morabity brothers who run gazelle-like over the sand. So many fast trail runners out here, some of the best in the world. Almost everyone looks the same in their desert gear, which is why the stormtrooper stands out. Chris Sparrow is British. He has run this race twice before. Now he has returned to the Sahara in full *Star Wars* gear to raise money for charity. His white helmet alone weighs 2kg. I cannot imagine running in that helmet and body armour in this heat. It won't be that long before he realises it was a big mistake. He at least has running shoes and gaiters on, unlike a Japanese man who's walking towards us in traditional Japanese wooden clogs. His flat wooden sandals, called *geta*, are raised up off the ground by two pieces of wood. A flip-flop-style thong holds his feet in place. He's flanked by another Japanese man dressed as an aubergine and a Japanese woman who's got a huge strawberry costume over her head.

Patrick Bauer is bouncing around on the roof of a Land Rover Defender playing an air guitar. AC/DC's 'Highway to Hell' – the soundtrack to this race – is blasting out across the desert. Everyone is now smiling, packed in together, jumping up and down. The atmosphere is electric. I have trained so hard for this. Now it is time to go. One foot in front of the other. Let's see how far I get.

'Good luck,' we all say to each other. A quick hug. *Quatre – trois – deux – un*. Cheers and whoops and AC/DC and helicopters, the noise is intense as we run over the start line. It is 9 a.m. and already warm. The April sun is lifting high above us. My backpack feels very heavy with all my water now on board. Despite Susie's assurances that today would be mostly running on dried-up riverbeds and not too difficult, within 3 miles or so it's already getting very soft underfoot, energy-sapping sand that seems to swallow up my feet. I wonder why I didn't bother to train on sand. The most I did was a couple of runs up and down the sandy horse trails in London's Hyde Park.

We slow to a walk on the first climb, and I have time now to look out across the desert. It is not how I had imagined it at all. It is vastly more beautiful, immense, dramatic, with huge skies, rolling dunes, mountains called *jebels* rising up in the distance. A few trees, some scrubby bushes, clumps of desert grasses, thorn heads all over the ground. No birds though, no animals, not even bugs. Nothing else is visible. Just us moving out here, the extreme runners dressed in strange gear. One of my biggest fears before this race had been getting lost and wandering alone in the desert. I realise quickly that this is not going to happen. I am in the middle of a snaking line of a thousand people following each other's heels. We are already very spread out. But I can see runners ahead and behind me for miles.

The heat is rising. It's such a dry heat that I hardly realise I am sweating until I fiddle with a strap on my rucksack and touch my back near the base of my spine. It is soaking. When we arrive at the first checkpoint 6 miles in, the race crew thrust bags of salt pills at us. We have to take at least 20 salt pills a day to make up for all the salt we are losing through sweat. 'Take at least one tablet every half hour,' one of the race team tells me as he hands me two bottles of water. The most we are allowed at each checkpoint is 3 litres. I refill the water bottles in my backpack and pour the rest over my head.

'I thought you said there weren't many sand dunes today, Susie,' I shout out, groaning. We are almost four hours into this race and I have done a lot of climbing up and running down enormous golden dunes now.

There are shouts from runners ahead and lots of pointing. They've seen the next camp, just a mile or so away. I have managed to run this stage with Susie, Shaun and

Tim, all of us taking it in turns to lead our little group, following each other's heels. We pass under the inflatable finish line in exactly the same time: 18.8 miles in 4 hours, 15 minutes. A live webcam has been set up at the finish for people tracking runners from home. I wave at it madly, wondering if Richard and the children are there watching online to see me run in. I'm not sure they'll recognise me in my desert gear even if they are. We are handed a small cup of mint tea, more water and more poo bags. And then we head off to find our tent.

Camp life is almost as important as the race itself. Your tent becomes your world. It is where you go as soon as you cross the finish line; same tent, same tentmates, even though the camp has now moved. It's where you recover, eat and fall asleep as soon as the sun goes down. There's no phone signal. Almost no contact with the outside world. Life becomes very simple. You exist in a bubble, surviving on freeze-dried food and a lot of laughter. There is nowhere to wash. No running water. Before the race I had imagined myself wandering through camp in those flip-flops I'd insisted on bringing, meeting runners from all over the world, chatting in French to the organisers and making new friends. Now that I am here, I do not move.

A change of clothes is one of the few luxuries Susie has allowed me. The shortest of shorts and the lightest of tops that I wriggle into in my sleeping bag. I use my penknife to turn an empty water bottle into the most basic of washing machines. I cut off the top third of the bottle, squeeze my sweat-soaked running kit inside with some water and then jam the rest of the bottle back on and shake it around. I don't even have soap. That would have been extra weight to carry. My clothes dry fast on the tent ropes. Meanwhile, my flip-flops are quickly adopted by the entire tent. Everyone borrows them, including Susie, to walk to the loo.

Every evening as we are settling down for the night there is a ripple of excitement as a head torch bobs towards us. It is the 'desert postman', one of the race crew out in the darkness popping into every tent bringing us all messages that have been emailed from home. Susie, who's got a big following on social media, gets pages and pages of them. She has told everyone she is out here and thrives on the pressure of making her challenge public. Hardly anyone knows I am here, so my messages are just from family and very close friends. 'Mum, I caught 3 fish. You are soooooooooooo crazy doing this. Hope you come back alive. From Ollie,' says my 10-year-old son. 'Hi mummy! You are amazing and so so so crazy at the same time! However well you do, we are all so proud of you!' types 12-year-old Georgie. 'Well done Soph,' writes my husband. 'We were following you. One step at a time. You can do it.' 'My mission accomplished… now it's your turn,' writes our nanny Mimi, who I realise must have just conquered the Great Wall of China. 'ENJOY IT, DO IT and DIG DEEP… words that you have said to me and that got me through last week!' The typo in my 13-year-old's message makes me laugh: 'Hi Mum! You did amazing today! I'm not going to tell you that we miss you because I don't want you to feel bad. You can't do it mum. Love Ella xxx' It is strange being given words from the outside world. This is a one-way postal service.

## Day two
## 39km (24.2 miles)
## 448m (1470 feet) of climbing

My self-inflating sleeping mat bursts on the first night. I wake up on a hard floor. It takes me a moment or two to realise that there's no longer anything soft between me and the stony desert ground. 'I did warn you,' says Susie, watching me try to inflate my mat again and hearing the hiss of air. 'There are really sharp thorn heads everywhere.' She is sleeping on an egg crate camping pad, the lightest you can get of course. It had looked horribly uncomfortable until now. I probably should have listened to her after all. This though is not the moment to worry about any of this. I've got to heat up water for my breakfast and then repack my bag for another long day ahead.

We shuffle back to the start line on stiff legs. We get a thumbs up from the Japanese man in wooden clogs who is still going, along with the Strawberry and the Aubergine. The Stormtrooper isn't here though. He was airlifted out of camp last night with chest pains, we are told. Apparently, he wanted to keep going.

Ahead of us is a day of rocky climbs, long, flat plains and then a steep *jebel* that we will have to haul ourselves up and over. My legs don't feel as tired as I was expecting when we start running again. The mountain we must climb is visible from miles away. The journey there seems interminable, a long line of runners snaking out in front of us across this stony, baked ground. At the base of the *jebel* is another checkpoint where we drink, down some snacks and throw water over our heads in preparation for the big climb. It's much steeper than I expected, with huge slabs of rock that we have to pick our way through, gasping for air in the heat. I pull my running poles out of my backpack to steady myself as we climb. We are rewarded with sweeping, magnificent views from the top, where for the first time I get a real sense of the ruggedness and scale of the Sahara. The climb is worth it too for the cooling breeze on the summit and the spectacular descent back down to the valley floor. It is so steep that there's a rope to hold on to in case we are worried about falling. This side of the mountain is not covered in rocks. Instead, it's golden sand, and the temptation to run down it at full pelt is overwhelming. We descend quickly one after the other, shrieking with laughter, kicking up waves of sand as our feet disappear into the spongy ground beneath us. Some lose their footing and tumble down head over heels but the ground is so soft they just jump up again and keep going. The next camp is visible in the distance. It's still about 5 miles away. But we can now make out the black circles of tents at the bivouac. It is a welcome sight after almost 20 miles on our feet.

Back at camp all the talk is of the 'long stage' in two days' time. It looms large over us all: 53.6 miles in one go that will either make or completely break us. I try not to listen to the fretting, focusing instead on my more immediate concerns – my feet and my food.

In the tent next door to us, there is a lot of food. A Notting Hill estate agent called Oli is in there with three of his friends from the Army and we soon realise that they have brought too much to eat. Their backpacks are incredibly heavy. Somehow, they have also managed to secure an eight-man tent for just four of them. The estate agent's doing, we all say. What it means is that there is plenty of room for us all when we manage to summon up the energy to pop next door. Which is something we do increasingly, the hungrier we get, eyeing up their food. We are surviving on very little out here. Three thousand calories a day for this race is not nearly enough for me, and I can tell I have already lost weight.

Our neighbours may have enough food and space but they haven't mastered their feet. Nick, who is ex-Army, is carrying a huge backpack and he is wearing shoes that are too big. After more than 40 miles of desert running, the soles of his feet are already badly blistered and bandaged up. He becomes a familiar figure at 'Doc Trotters' in camp, which is where you go when your feet are in trouble. Every afternoon, a trail of runners forms up ant-like outside the tent where volunteers wielding scalpels slice the tops off blisters and drip iodine into open wounds. I can hear people shouting out in pain. As the days pass, the number of runners in camp with their feet swaddled in white bandages grows, until many of them look like they've been mummified beneath the knees. I marvel at their determination to keep going despite the excruciating wounds on their feet.

The medical tent is also busy. One of our tentmates, Jon, has been put on an intravenous drip after pushing too hard in the heat. He had stumbled over the finish line and then vomited a lot. I go to see him. I feel a little guilty. Jon is a friend of my husband's, an England squash player. A good athlete. A year ago, he had popped over to our house for a quick cup of tea and I told him what I was training for in the desert. He was fascinated. 'You should come!' I said. He left our house 20 minutes later and signed up too. Now he is lying here, looking wrecked. *This is my fault*, I think to myself. Plenty of others around him are in the same state – fevered, confused. The rules say two bags of fluid are allowed to rehydrate. Any more than that and you're out of the race. Jon has one bag, then two. He is so determined not to be sent home that he asks me to go and fetch his friend, Jamie, to get him out of there. He looks ashen when he returns to our tent. There's no way he's going to make it to the start line tomorrow, we all think.

### Day three
### 31.6km (19.6 miles)
### 738m (2421 feet) of climbing

Sunrise reveals a camp transformed. It is the morning after the huge sandstorm that had swept through the bivouac, depriving us all of much-needed sleep. Finally, it has stopped, and we crawl out from beneath the collapsed canopy of our tent. I can see straight into the middle of camp now, through gaps where tents have been flattened, leaving jagged edges like missing teeth. At least half of the camp seems to have been blown over. Dazed runners move slowly around, searching for lost belongings. Socks, jackets, sleeping mats that have cartwheeled off into the desert are unlikely to be found. Those who have lost precious kit are asking around for spare clothes. How will they continue running without it? We are carrying the bare minimum already to keep our backpacks light. 'I told you to put everything away at night,' Susie keeps saying, even though I have lost nothing, so I can continue. Tim, who'd been exposed to the full force of the storm, has lost a spare jacket but, it turns out, not his socks. He found them this morning, stuffed down into the bottom of his sleeping bag. He can run on.

A slow, tired procession is moving towards today's start line. Jon is with us, revived after his spell in the medical tent it seems. Patrick Bauer is up there on top of the Land Rover again. The music is blaring out 'Highway to Hell'. We jig around, almost dancing, giddy with a lack of sleep. Next to me a man is missing one of his yellow gaiters needed to keep the sand out of his shoes. I don't fancy his chances. He will be in need of the medics at Doc Trotters by the time we reach the next camp.

Stage three is all about climbing. We have two *jebels* to scale. One is so steep we will need to pull ourselves up through rocks and sand using a rope. The climb on to the first ridge is like scaling a giant sand dune. My feet keep slipping from under me, sinking deep with each step. There's no clear path marked, just a long line of runners, and some are veering off to the left, trying to find a more gentle ascent to the top. Once we are up there, the view is unbelievable. The *jebel* we are on drops off steeply on either side to vast plateaus, edged in the distance by more mountains. It stretches on for miles and miles. Martian-like. They make films about being on Mars out here, someone near me is saying. The only moving creatures are us. Ungainly, unsteady in this heat. What other wildlife would willingly expose itself to these conditions? Creatures with sense don't come out in this burning heat. They remain buried in cool places.

We start running along the ridge, a narrow path strewn with rocks. I watch my feet but keep trying to look up to appreciate the view. After a few miles there is a steep drop. We fly down it, arms out, running on air, desert hats flapping, laughing like children, springing in and out of the spongy sand on another exhilarating descent to the desert floor. In the far distance, on the plateau, a trail of tiny figures is marching ant-like towards the next checkpoint 5 miles away.

Jebel El Otfal is the mountain that Susie has been dreading. This woman who will run 100-mile races, cross deserts and jungles, and push herself to the absolute limit, is frightened of heights. The climb of more than a mile is so steep that there's a rope nailed into the rocks to help us scale it. 'The first time I went up this in 2013,' she warns me as we're running towards it, 'I completely froze. I just couldn't move and I was on my own. People were getting really cross because they couldn't get past me. It took me absolutely ages to get up it. If I freeze, Soph, you've got to give me a shove, get me up there.'

It is even steeper than I was expecting, a 25 per cent gradient and we have to clamber over huge boulders holding on to the rope. I stay behind Susie and feel her fear setting in. She hesitates. I cajole her. I reassure her and urge her on. In the end I just have to put my hand on her bottom and give her an almighty shove up. She yelps, then we laugh and we continue like that until we reach the top, though at one point she gets so scared, I think she's going to hit me. And it's not over yet. The drop down on the other side is just as steep, rocky, technical and difficult. There is a constant fear of tripping.

The final stretch to the next camp is 6 miles over a plateau. We march; we don't run. I trail behind Susie, Shaun and Tim. We are all still together. No one speaks. I wasn't sure I would manage to make it to the end of Stage one of the Marathon des Sables. Now I have almost completed Stage three. But tomorrow will be the real test.

## Day four
## 86.2km (53.6 miles)
## 1254m (4114 feet) of climbing

'Six more hours to go,' says Tim, unhelpfully pointing off into the dusky distance. This is not information that I need to hear. We left our last camp almost 10 hours ago at the start of this 53.6-mile run. We still have more than 25 miles to go. The sun is going down behind us now. We are all exhausted. We will be running in the dark soon.

The first 10 miles or so that morning had been across more rocky dried-up riverbeds and then into the El Maharch pass, a leafy, verdant oasis of palm trees, people and homes that surprised us after so many days of sand and rock. Our path was lined with our first race spectators, children high-fiving us and handing out bright pink flowers plucked from oleander bushes behind them. One boy tried to sell us a lizard.

Then we were off out the other side and on to salt plains as the heat rose quickly around us. It would hit almost 50°C that day. We fell into a fast, steady march, climbing up on to soft terracotta-coloured sand that stretched on as far as the eye could see: 360-degree views. It looked like a film set. Rocky escarpments rising in the distance, scrubby bushes along our way, barren plateaus below us. The desert colours all the more vivid set against the bright blue of the cloudless sky. On and on we went, lurching from checkpoint to checkpoint, seven in total over the 53.6 miles. As we closed in on Checkpoint 4 late in the afternoon, we found one of the Army boys from the next-door tent bent over double being sick in the sand. He was overheating. A train of wild camels appeared in the distance. Twelve of them moving slowly in the opposite direction. My feet were hurting a lot now and I was so hungry. We had not had a proper meal since breakfast. How could we survive six more hours of this?

It's dark by the time we reach Checkpoint 5 or 'CP5', as it's known. This is a legendary stop during the MDS and it is bigger than all the other checkpoints. There are deckchairs, plenty of tents, sometimes even musicians play here. Many runners will bed down at this checkpoint for the night and continue the race at dawn. The cut-off time for the long stage is generous and we don't have to complete it until 5 p.m. tomorrow afternoon. But many, like us, want to get it all done in one go so that we can have the whole day off tomorrow. The race organisers will give us a can of Coca-Cola in camp on rest day. We are clinging on for our sugary treat.

In the tent where we shelter and finally boil water to make some proper food, a Norwegian man is talking gibberish. He looks utterly exhausted, disorientated and is not making sense. There are plenty of medics here. They won't let him set off again like this. We are all ragged now and the lure of this tent is strong. Susie is struggling and starts wondering out loud whether she can go on. It is extraordinary that she is out here at all given her operations just two months ago. I eat my freeze-dried macaroni cheese in the light of my head torch. It is delicious and warm.

---

Four small circles of light move slowly across the sand. Our head torches create a golden path in the black night. I have never run in the dark like this before. It is mesmerising. The world closes in to just my feet, the sand slipping beneath them, the sound of my breath. To the left, to the right, deep black. Behind us I can still see the lights from Checkpoint 5. In front of us, in the far-off distance, the bobbing lights from the head torches of a handful of other runners, snaking over endless dunes, reminding us just how far we still have to go. Above us, the vast, extraordinary canopy of stars. So many pinpricks of light.

It is 11 p.m. and we have decided to push on. We want our day of rest tomorrow and our can of Coke before the final day of this race: a marathon run to the finish line and our medals. We follow a sparse path of fluorescent green batons laid out every quarter of a mile or so to ensure we don't get lost. I wouldn't like to be out here on my own.

Susie, Shaun, Tim and I have managed to stay together since the first day, running at roughly the same pace and taking it in turns to drive each other on. 'Here comes the Cavalcade!' people have started shouting as they see us pass. Now, though, I am struggling to stay with them. For the first time I want to cry. There are three more hours ahead of us. I don't know how I can carry on. A creature with a long tail scurries through our torchlight: 'A desert gerbil,' someone shouts. It momentarily lifts my spirits. But I sink back quickly into the dark hole in my mind. This is the worst I have felt in the entire race. Rock bottom. We are on sand dunes now that slip away in the darkness beneath my feet. I fall behind. Shaun notices and slows right down to walk beside me. He doesn't say a word but his presence is so reassuring and keeps me going. It's the kindest gesture. I am having to dig very deep right now. 'Shaun The Rock. Thank you,' I mumble, smiling. We frogmarch on and on silently. I listen to the *click click click* of my poles. An endless metronome.

We reach camp at two in the morning, jogging silently over the finish line together. Mint tea in small cups is poured out from a silver teapot and handed to us. We limp slowly to tent 128 and finally collapse into our sleeping bags in a sweaty, dirty heap. What I would do right now for a shower. Two of our tentmates, Jamie and Jon, are already here, fast asleep. The others won't arrive until tomorrow lunchtime. They had decided to sleep at Checkpoint 5. So, for the first time in almost a week, we can spread out a bit. 'Only one more marathon to go now,' whispers Susie. 'We have broken the back of it. You must realise now you can do this?' I shake my head slowly. 'I won't believe I can do it until it is done,' I whisper back. 'There's still a long, long way to go.' And then finally, I am asleep.

## Day five
### Rest day

A lie-in at last. I dream of a big breakfast. A whole day with nothing to do, except recover. The stoves are being lit around me. Screeches from a nearby tent. Someone has seen a scorpion and is chasing it out. The tent banter begins, with the tales of other people's adventures last night in the dunes. We think of our missing tentmates, still out there on the course. Our estate agent neighbour Oli will hopefully be with them, getting it done at last. Already we can hear people clapping the early morning arrivals. I am so glad we pushed on last night.

Food trading begins. It is fun and it is thrilling. We are all excited by the prospect of getting something to eat that we didn't bring. I've had the same 1000-calorie freeze-dried stodgy porridge every day. I swap it with Susie for a packet of freeze-dried muesli instead. A sachet of instant coffee is traded in for a Yorkshire tea bag. A chunk of vacuum-packed Parmesan is passed over for a handful of cashew nuts.

I haven't showered or changed my clothes for five days now. I peel off my two pairs of socks to find out what the long stage has done to my feet. It is not pretty. Susie orders me to dry them in the sun. I lie on my back, half in, half out of the tent, to see what a bit of sunshine and dry heat will do to the blisters on several toes. My feet are not as bad as many others'. Jon, in our tent, looks like he has been mummified. No skin is now visible. Just bandages on show. But it's Nick, in the tent next door, whose feet are the worst. The soles of his feet are red, raw and bloody. Very little is intact. He can barely walk. We all wonder how he will make it to the end.

A woman from the race team arrives with the cans of Coca-Cola. Small cans but they are cold. It is the first cold thing I have had all week. She gives us half a packet of tissues too. We can't believe our luck. Even loo paper is now scarce, a highly prized commodity round here.

At the end of the day, just before 5 p.m., we head back to the finish. It is a tradition of this race that the whole camp comes out to applaud those bringing up the rear. The last to arrive is a British man in his 70s, bent over, leaning heavily to one side, in terrible pain as he staggers over the line. He has made it just inside the cut-off time. The two camels bringing up the rear are visible behind him. The whole camp shouts and cheers as Patrick Bauer goes over to greet him. I can't imagine how he is going to be able to recover in time to set off again on the final marathon tomorrow.

## Day six
## 42.2km (26.2 miles)
## 505m (1657 feet) of climbing

We wake up in another sandstorm. It's not as bad as the one that flattened camp a few days ago. But the wind is strong and the sand swirls violently around us as we gather at the start for the last time. We all pull our buffs right over our faces, only our sunglasses now visible, as we wait for the final countdown. And then we are off. The upside to this sandstorm is that the heat has gone. It's only about 22°C today and the wind makes it feel even cooler still. I can scent the finish now. The excitement builds. As the hours pass, I speed up, running down the sand dunes, marching up the other side. After more than a year of training and fretting and sweat-filled panic, I know I will do this now, even if I won't say that to the others.

My running watch, which somehow is still going, says there are just 7 miles left. That's my normal river run at home. Now I really pick up the pace. So much so that I have to stop and wait for the others in an abandoned village with less than 3 miles to go. I can't finish without them all now. 'Almost there! *Presque là!*' shout some of the race crew in high-vis vests standing in the shady ruins.

The four of us join hands and lift our arms high over our heads as we approach the finish. Runners, wrapped in their national flags, are zigzagging in celebration towards the end. Patrick Bauer is there beaming, holding armfuls of medals. He hands them all out himself. So many people cry. Sob even. I'm one of them. I stand there speechless, tears rolling down my dirty, salty skin. I cannot believe I have got to the end. 'What did I tell you?' says Susie, giving me a massive hug. 'You are so, so much stronger than you think.'

My mobile phone is still alive, just. There's one bar of battery. I call my family to let them know I've done it and then collapse in the tent. 'Can I tell people you're out here now?' says Susie, looking hopeful. She has been keeping this secret for so long. I contemplate putting a photo of my medal on Twitter, revealing my desert adventure at last. My thumb hovers over 'post' and then I decide not to. Not yet. I want to keep it just for me for a little bit longer out here in my desert bubble. I've done it. My own amazement is enough.

I relent finally a few hours later. '6 marathons in 5 days – 150 miles across the Sahara Desert carrying all my food and kit for the week. Was so terrified I didn't tell anyone I was doing @marathonDsables! But I just finished it' I tweet. A wave of disbelief flows through my phone. I don't dare open any of the messages because my battery is about to run out, but I can see the top lines as they pour in. Even Andy Murray sends me a message with clapping hand emojis. 'Andy Murray' just sent me a message! THE Andy Murray,' I yelp to Susie. And then my phone battery finally dies.

That evening there is a party. We have one more night in camp and we still have to feed ourselves even though the race is done. But we do get given a can of beer each and it is cold. Camp is cold too now as the wind whips around us. We stand huddled upright, like cold penguins, sleeping bags wrapped around our shoulders for warmth. The prize-giving is held on the back of a lorry. We are all giddy with relief. No prizes for the Cavalcade but we have finished in the top third of the pack after a total of 39 hours in the race. Susie and I are 26th and 27th women. I've managed to finish third in my age group. Already my mind is whirring. Could I do it again, faster next time? More than 900 have finished the race. Just over 100 had to drop out, including the man in his 70s who we had watched come in last night. He made it to the very last checkpoint today, before the medics hauled him off, judging it not safe for him to go on. Brutal after all that effort. One of the final runners to cross the line was the Japanese man in his wooden clogs.

## Day seven
## 7.7km (4.8 miles)
## 104m (341 feet) of climbing

Running water, a shower, proper food. They are all just hours away now. Tonight we will be in a five-star hotel sleeping on beds, not the tent floor. But first we have to walk out of the desert to the nearest town, just 5 miles away. We are handed new T-shirts, blue with the MDS charity logo on the front. Clean clothes, the first clean clothes I have had for a week. Nick, our tent neighbour, is high on painkillers. He has lost most of the skin on the soles of his feet now. Drugs are the only way he is going to make it out of here. He won't give up.

The further out of the desert we walk, the closer other humans come. Small luxury camps appear for tourists. We see quad bikes and camels and people surfing down dunes. A strange contrast to the wilderness we have inhabited for more than a week. In town there are coaches waiting to take us on the six-hour journey back to Ouarzazate and our hotel. We will spend two more nights there 'decompressing' with all the British runners before heading to the airport and flying out. Susie, an old hand at this race now, marches past the coaches with us following in her wake.

She finds a taxi driver who agrees to take us to Ouarzazate, with a stop for food on the way. A real meal, with bread. Lots of it. I am so hungry. I can tell I have lost quite a lot of weight. The driver has barely left town before he has wound all of the windows in the taxi right down. Only then do we all realise just how much we must stink.

The Berbère Palace in Ouarzazate is where he takes us. It is a luxury five-star hotel behind huge wooden doors with lush green gardens and a glistening azure swimming pool. The first thing we are told is that we are not allowed in the pool. We can sit by it, but we cannot swim in it at all. They must know about the state of our feet. My hair, thick with sand and grease, stands in big rigid mounds on top of my head when I finally take my ponytail out for the first time in more than a week. None of it moves. I step into the shower. Running water at last. And then I screech because large clumps of my hair are coming out in my hands. I panic, thinking it must be a result of the stress I have just put my body through in the desert. Have I triggered major hair loss? 'Oh my God,' I shout to Susie, who's in the next room. 'My hair's falling out!' I hear her laugh. 'Don't panic! You've had it tied up all week,' she shouts back through the door. 'Totally normal! It's all the hair that would have naturally fallen out if you'd had it down.'

They say you return from the Marathon des Sables a different person. I hadn't really believed that before. But I did now. Physically I was a lot lighter, having lost more than a stone in just one week. Mentally I was a lot tougher. I understood for the first time that my body really was so much stronger than my mind had let me believe. I had arrived in the Sahara full of fear and with little confidence.

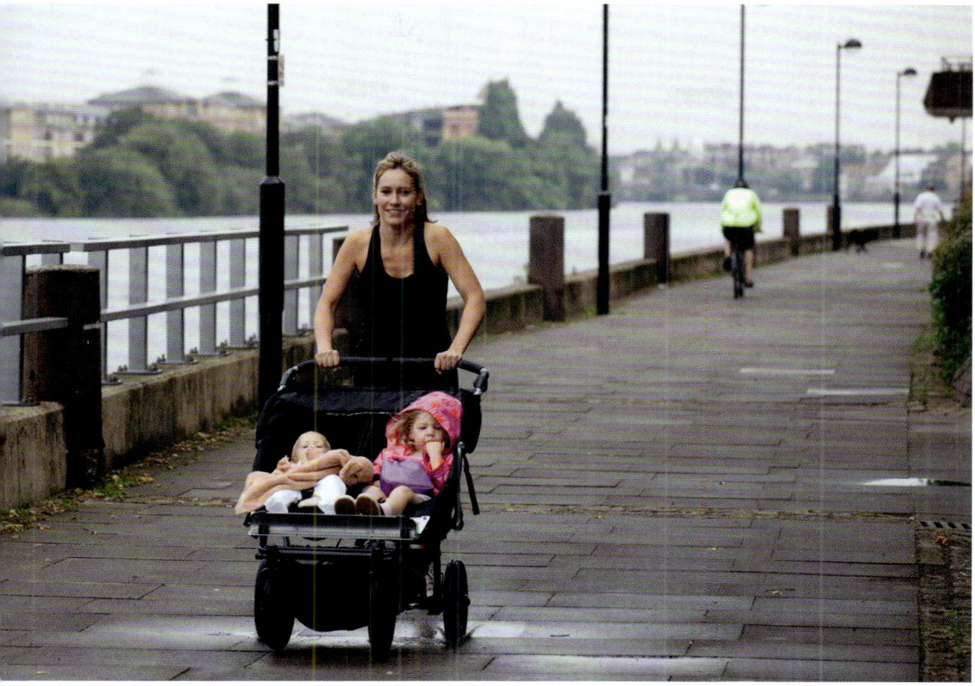

Andrew Crowley, *The Telegraph*

ning for the Great North Run 2006 with Georgie and Ella

Marathon-Photos.com

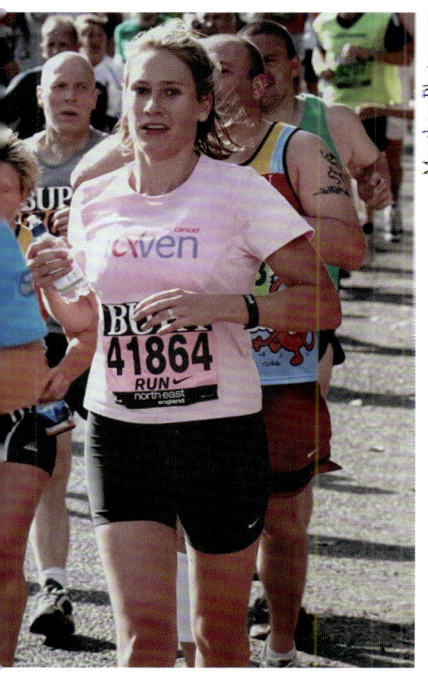

t race at the Great North Run 2006

Arsenal blow it
Title hopes dashed in final seconds SPORT S2&3

Telegraph Selected
Top theatre tickets less than half price SEE PAGES 2&19

# The Daily Telegraph

Monday, April 18, 2011 telegraph.co.uk

Councils 'cutting as they sit on millions'

Plucky Sophie's marathon tribute

Secrets put on internet in Whitehall blunders

Clearly there are issues which are sensitive. If they are supposed to be concealed then for God's sake conceal them

Cameron: AV would damage democracy

Cambridge beats Oxford to top spot in new rankings

Weather is set fair for Easter (unlike the M1)

BREITLING *for* BENTLEY

Dominic Lipinski, *The Telegraph*

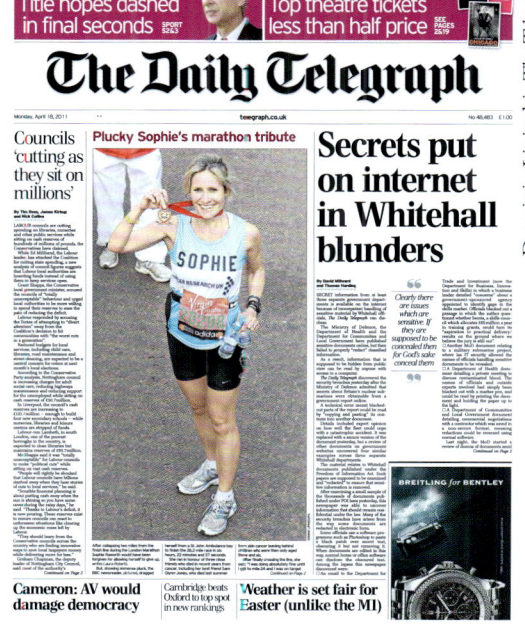

▲ Front page of the *Telegraph* in 2011 – I felt like I had failed

▲ Trinny and Susannah trying to dress me for their show *What Not to Wear on the Red Carpet*

▲ With Jeremy Bowen in 2000, when he joined BBC *Breakfast News*

▼ With George Alagiah launching the new *Six O'Clock News* in 2003

▲ George and Franny Alagiah in 2014 with my Boston medal that he kept with him during the first two years of his cancer treatment

Running the Boston Marathon in 2014
© Jacquie Millett / Boston Athletic Association

▲ Running the Tokyo Marathon in 2017
Author's collection

◀ Shortly after Dad was diagnosed with Parkinson's in 2016, I ran the London Marathon to raise money for charity. He took this photo as I finished
Author's collection

▲ With Susie at the Berlin Marathon 2016
Berlin Marathon/MarathonFoto

◀ With the gang at the Chicago Marathon 2017 (clockwise: me, Shaun, Tim, Emily, Sam and Susie)
Author's collection

◀ By our tent the day before the Marathon des Sables race started, wearing all the kit I had to carry

▲ Savouring the last moments on my inflatable mattress befor heading out on the race

▲ Powering through sand dunes

▲ The MDS finish line with Susie and Shaun, and our med

Man v Horse 2018 – racing ses across the Welsh mountains

▲ With Sir Brendan Foster at the Great North Run in 2018

▼ Learning to lift heavy

◀ Running across the Alps in the 35-mile OCC race to Chamonix in 2022

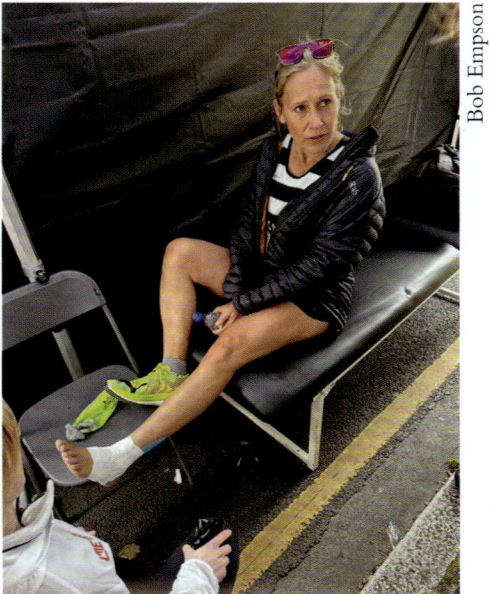

▲ St John Ambulance station at mile 20 of the London Marathon in April 2024

▲ With my wonderful father Richard Raworth in 2018

▲ Richmond parkrun friends including Sally (kneeling), Mike (right-hand-side bike) and Serge (next to Mike in white)

▲ Arriving at Downing Street on Election Results Day in July 2024

▲ About to go on air for the *BBC News at Six*

▲ Waiting to present the *BBC News at Six* from Bayeux Cemetery in Normandy with my army-supplied crutches

▲ Life on a knee scooter – complete with a glass of rosé in the cup holder

▲ One of my favourite Isle of Wight runs with a view of the Needles

▲ Running with Luna in Sussex

▲ Adventures along the Thames Path near Dartford crossing – 60 miles to go until the sea!

▲ The end of my 232-mile run from the source of the Thames in Gloucestershire to the North Sea

I was leaving it feeling more fulfilled than I had for many years. The challenge, the simplicity of life, the friendships and bonds, the months of training and preparation it had taken me just to get here. I had pushed myself to my absolute limit out there in the desert. I had been stripped back to my very core, completely exposed, revealing depths and reserves I did not know I had. I had also discovered the freedom and joy of running off-grid.

# 7
## *Galloping to a place on the podium*

'Horse! Horse!' someone is shouting in the distance. 'Horse! Big horse!' The cries are getting closer now, rippling along the path towards us. I can hear its hooves thudding the ground as it closes in. 'Horse!' someone shouts again. I don't dare look back, but it sounds like it is right behind me now. Suddenly a flash of orange as the great beast canters past – orange flecks on its hooves, an orange bobble on the rider's hat. A big horse and a colour co-ordinated one at that. It was so close I could have touched it. 'Horse! Horse!' people shout again. This time I stop and step off the narrow track to let another one pass. 'This horse needs more space,' shouts its rider, looming over us. I'm not sure if she's angry or not. It's hard for us to get out of the way. She canters past, without seeming to slow down at all. Both horses fly off through the forest ahead of us. I step back on to the track and laugh. This is Man V Horse and it is already the funniest race I have ever run.

We had gathered that morning in the smallest town in Wales, Llanwrtyd Wells in Powys, between the Cambrian mountains and the Brecon Beacons. The town may be tiny with a population of around 800 people, but it has been put firmly on the map by the man who for years was the landlord of the Neuadd Arms Hotel in the middle of it. In 1980, Gordon Green was talking to the local Master of the Hunt in the back bar of the hotel. Gordon had just been to the Lake District where the terrain is so mountainous that hunting with hounds on horseback is impossible. For centuries the huntsmen had accompanied the hounds on foot. 'That is what you should be doing here,' Gordon told the Master in Llanwrtyd Wells. 'You should use runners instead of horses.' 'And that's how this race began,' he tells me decades later, sitting in the bar where that conversation took place. 'We decided to test out what would be faster over a long distance on this terrain around here, a man or a horse?' Gordon was convinced that a man could beat a horse as long as the distance was far enough. In June that year, he put it to the test. Forty runners and eight horses from nearby villages set off from outside the Neuadd Arms on a 20-mile race across the Welsh hills for what was the inaugural Man V Horse. The horse won. By a long way. It beat the fastest runner by almost three-quarters of an hour. But Gordon Green remained confident. The race became an annual event with a £1000 prize on offer for the first man or woman to beat a horse and prove Gordon right. The prize money rolled over year after year. Which is how Huw Lobb, an experienced cross-country runner who had narrowly missed out on Olympic marathon selection, won £25,000 in 2004. He took on the horses and beat them all, finishing in 2 hours, 5 minutes and 11 seconds. He had just 2 minutes to spare before the lead horse galloped in.

Now, many years later, in June 2018, fresh back from the Sahara, Susie, Shaun and I are standing outside the Neuadd

Arms with more than 700 runners getting ready to race over 40 horses and riders. The Olympic 400-metre runner, Iwan Thomas, is with us too. He is doing a film about this race for the BBC's *One Show*. A lot of the runners who are milling about around us look rather like finely tuned racehorses themselves: lithe, long limbs, strong, mostly men. This race is fell runners' territory. There are a lot of steep climbs and even steeper descents. None of it is flat. It'll be punishing on our legs with around 4000 feet (1200 metres) of climbing over 22 miles. A lot of it is run over private land and so they change the route and distance slightly every year depending on whose land they can use.

The hotel is thronging with runners, a lot of them queuing down a steep staircase for the loo. On the walls of this place where the race was born are bits of memorabilia, photos of past races, lots of horses and boards with the names of all the winners over the years. And in among it all, the man himself. Eighty-three-year-old Gordon Green is no longer the landlord, but he is a legend in this town. Not only did he come up with Man V Horse, he also launched the World Bog Snorkelling Championships, which take place here every year too, at the end of August. That is not a race I will ever compete in. The bog snorkellers have to swim two lengths of a murky 50m ditch that has been cut into a bog nearby. They swim face down, wearing flippers but with no normal swim strokes allowed. It is essentially doggy paddle in a boggy ditch with a mask and snorkel while being yelled at by huge crowds.

Our race is due to start at 11 a.m. With 15 minutes to go, we stand tightly packed at the start outside the hotel and watch our competition arrive. It's like a weigh-in at a much-hyped boxing match, with the two sides squaring up to each other. The runners are on one side of the road, the spectators are on the other side behind barriers. In between us all, the horses and riders appear, trotting skittishly through the crowds. We clap and cheer. They wave and smile from on high. Not long now until we take each other on. And Gordon Green was right. This race is not always as predictable as you'd think. It depends very much on the weather and how dry the ground is. The runners are given a 15-minute head start, mainly to avoid us all being trampled by hooves on narrow paths. What that means is that at the end of the race, once the first runner comes in, there'll be a nail-biting 15 minutes to wait to find out if horse or man (or woman) wins.

We are about 5 miles into the race before the first horses appear. A shiny chestnut mare passes us on one of the wide fire roads that criss-cross this mountain. Her rider waves and gives us a thumbs up as they canter by. We turn into the forest where the path is narrow and the branches hang low. More horses start streaming past. We throw ourselves into the trees at times just to get out of the way. Given the number of horses that pass us, you'd think there would be no contest. But when we finally climb out on to open moorland, where the skylarks are singing, 11 miles into the race, the horses all have to stop to be checked by vets. They are unsaddled, sponged down, given some 'recovery mash' – dried feed soaked in water – and the riders must wait until their horse's heart rate is 60 beats per minute or below before they can set off again. It can take at least half an hour, often longer. Then the vet will check them over, making them trot up and down. Once the vet is happy, they're allowed to canter on and chase down more runners. Some horses won't get back on the course at all. There are no such checks for us humans. We are all just waved on.

Horses will always beat humans over short distances but over longer stretches man does have a chance, particularly when it's hot or the ground is muddy, and the horses and riders are worried about slipping. 'In the animal kingdom,' Gordon had told me before we set off, 'runners will always beat whatever animal it is over a certain distance. That animal will have to stop, whether it's a cheetah, probably the first to stop, or a gazelle and so on. It is a scientific fact.' Today it is a warm June day, temperatures are rising, and after recent rain the ground is soft, which means a tricky combination for the big beasts. The horses are good on the gentler ascents, but we catch them on the steeper downhills. We laugh and spar with the riders as we play a version of cat and mouse. Mountain streams provide cool relief for us all. I stand ankle-deep at one crossing, throwing water over my head and body, only to find myself eye to eye with a horse that has decided to stop right next to me for a drink.

'Just 3 miles to go,' shouts a volunteer as I throw myself up yet another hill. 'Less than a parkrun,' I shout to no one in particular as I pass another two horses that have been reduced to a walk. Susie should have been with me but she dropped back miles ago. A month after we ran across the Sahara, she flew to Florida to run 100 miles along the Florida Keys all in one go. She finished in just under 26 hours. 'You've had cancer. You've had two operations. You've run across the Sahara. Now you're going to run a 100-miler?' I had yelped when she told me her plans. 'Are you mad?' But of course, she did it. It was a road event in the Florida heat with only one bend in the route. My idea of mental torture. That was only two weeks ago. Now the Welsh mountains have finally finished her off. Her legs have had enough. 'That was ridiculous, now I think of it,' she later says, laughing. 'I think I may have been overreaching at that point.'

The white tents at the finish line are visible from about a mile off and it is downhill all the way now. I leg it as fast I can, dodging small ditches and tree roots as I go. I have run most of this race on my own. I hadn't planned to but as the Sahara has taught me, I am stronger both physically and mentally than I think. I've always insisted on running races with friends who prop me up with much-needed psychological support. But now as I head towards the field in the valley where horses and runners are charging at the finish, I realise I can do this on my own. I check my running watch and see that I could get there in under 4 hours. Confidence soaring, I sprint to the end.

The field by the finish is like a village fete. All the talk is of this year's nail-biting race. Joe Dale, a runner from London, was first over the line, finishing in 2 hours, 35 minutes and 12 seconds. The horses had set off 14 minutes after us and so he had to stand there waiting with the excited crowds to see if he was about to become the third man in race history to beat all the horses. The tension grew. Still no sound of hooves. And then with one minute to go, when Joe must have thought he had done it, Ronnie the horse and Peter Davies the rider came galloping across the field. Thirty-five seconds was all that stood between Joe Dale and a £2500 prize. He lost it.

By the time I've heard the whole story, Shaun and Iwan Thomas come galloping towards the line, followed 5 minutes later by Susie. She's only half an hour behind me. She must have found a last-minute spurt of energy and is now waving and whooping at the crowd. In a large white marquee, a dozen or so ladies from the local community group are handing out free tea and sandwiches for all the shattered runners. There are so many sandwiches to choose from: egg mayonnaise, cheese and pickle, cucumber or tuna mayo. But their signature dish is the jam and cheese sandwich, which is surprisingly tasty. Two of the women, Susan and Delyth, who live in the town, have been doing the sandwiches for the runners since the race began 38 years ago. Susan, who's in her 70s, says they've been buttering up the bread for about five hours now since the runners and riders set off. She loves being part of this event. 'All you runners are so appreciative,' she says laughing. 'I meet people every year who tell me, obviously teasing, that the sandwiches are one of the big reasons why they do the race.' I reach for one of the famous cheese and jam sandwiches. 'We ran out of fillings one year and that was all we could offer them. It was a rather unusual mix. But they absolutely loved them, and we've been making them ever since!' We pile our plates high gratefully and wander off to find a place on the grass where we can stretch out in the sunshine.

Susie is mid-sentence when I suddenly leap up and stagger away on stiff legs. I have been lying in a semi daze listening to her chatting to Shaun while I watch more horses and runners appear. I am vaguely aware of a loudspeaker on the other side of the field. 'And the ... goes to Sophie Raworth,' I suddenly hear. To me? What does? What goes to me? I jump up and almost run. There's a small wooden podium in the field and they're handing out wooden trophies. 'Sophie! You *are* here! Well done. You were second in your over-45 age group. You also beat more than 20 horses.' I step up on to the podium, wincing.

It is still to this day the only trophy that I have ever won.

# 8

## *What about your knees?*

I am lying in an MRI scanner in London. For an hour and a half, I am not allowed to move. The machine whirrs and bangs as images are taken of every part of my knees, hips and pelvis. 'We are slicing you up like salami in a supermarket with our images,' I am told. If there's anything wrong, I'm going to know about it very soon. I have chosen to come here in the name of research. But ever since I said yes six weeks ago, I have been stricken by fear, convinced that I am going to be told that running 1500 miles a year in my 50s is damaging my ageing joints.

'What about your knees?' is the question I get asked all the time. Since I took up marathon running in 2011, my knees have mostly felt fine. I've had my fair share of injuries – mainly involving my Achilles, calves and a few other strained tendons. But my bones and joints have always felt like they're coping with the load. Recently, though, my knees have started making a strange crackling noise, like a crisp bag being crunched up, when I go upstairs. There's no pain at all but I can hear them if it's quiet and I find it increasingly disconcerting. Now as I lie here in this clanking, noisy scanner, I am bracing myself for bad news, wondering how I will cope if I am told today that my running days are over.

The man who is about to determine my fate with his scans is Professor Alister Hart, an orthopaedic surgeon, who for the past six years has been carrying out pioneering research into what running does to your hips and knees. We first met after I was invited to talk about running the Marathon des Sables at a doctors' conference in 2020. When it was time for questions, a hand shot up at the back of the auditorium. 'How are your knees?' boomed a voice in the semi-darkness, from a man whose face I couldn't quite see. I gulped and reeled backwards on stage in front of hundreds of doctors looking at me. 'Um, they're fine, I think,' I said nervously. 'Are you about to tell me they won't be?' The voice laughed. 'Not at all,' replied the man, who turned out to be Professor Hart. 'I've been scanning the knees and hips of hundreds of runners and cyclists. And from the research I've been doing, it does seem that all that running may not be doing your knees any harm. Quite the opposite in fact.'

Alister Hart's interest in running and knees was sparked after he finished his first marathon at the age of 42. For days afterwards, he limped around the Royal National Orthopaedic Hospital where he was working, clinging on to the side rails and shuffling up and down the stairs. His colleagues had little sympathy. 'Let's just say they weren't favourable to long-distance running,' he says, 'but it really got me thinking about what it was doing to my body.' And so, he began the largest and most detailed study of the knees of middle-aged marathon runners to date. He did MRI scans on the knees of 81 runners who were all in their 40s, all first-time marathon runners with no known injuries. Crucially, they all had to follow a 16-week marathon plan, building up slowly to race day. He wasn't sure what he would find. He did it with the help of the London Marathon organisers, something he now says was very brave of them to agree to. 'There was a risk we could have killed off running altogether with my research,' he says, smiling.

The results really surprised him. The runners were scanned six months before the 2017 London Marathon and then two weeks afterwards. Half of them were scanned again six months after that. In total he did MRIs on more than 400 knees. The first scans showed up abnormalities in almost all of their knees, issues they hadn't been aware of, like a partially torn meniscus or a tendon strain. But none of the abnormalities stopped any of them from finishing the marathon and the scans taken after the race showed no deterioration in their joints. What astonished Professor Hart even more was that they also found that the bones of some runners, whose first scans had shown up problems, had improved after the four-month training plan that culminated with the marathon. Changes in the bone marrow that had been seen on the first scans, often a sign of pre-arthritis, had completely vanished. 'It looks like the dose of running, even up to marathon level, is actually good for the bones. It strengthens them. And in turn that is good for the cartilage. That was a new finding. We really didn't expect that at all,' Alister tells me.

I have lost count of the number of people, almost always non-runners, who warn me of the damage I must be doing to my body. Osteoarthritis is the big fear, the thinning or loss of cartilage in your joints. 'Wear and tear' arthritis, as it is known, which then leads to increasing pain as bone rubs against bone. But Professor Hart has a new theory. He thinks 'wear and tear' arthritis needs to be renamed. Running strengthens our bones. That has been proven. Our skeleton needs to be stimulated by mechanical load, physical stress, like the impact from running or walking. And, says Professor Hart, we need strong bones to keep our cartilage healthy. 'If the bones are not supporting the cartilage, it gets damaged. That's one of the things that causes arthritis in the long term. I think "wear and tear" arthritis should be renamed as "inactivity" arthritis. It may actually be a lack of activity that leads to osteoarthritis. The more a joint is used, the stronger it makes the bone and muscle around it. Having healthy bone is crucial for healthy joints. It's a common fear, including among doctors, that taking up running will damage the joints. But it now looks like the opposite is true.'

More and more doctors and sports scientists are coming round to his way of thinking. Paul Hobrough is a running specialist physio, a man I first went to see when my Achilles flared up a few years after I started running. He had set up his own business in Teddington in South West London at the back of a Sweatshop running store that sold trainers. On Saturdays a young man called Mo Farah worked there to get some extra cash while he was running and studying at the local St Mary's University. Paul, a former Team GB elite flat-water kayaker, began to amass some of the top runners as his clients, from Paula Radcliffe and Mo Farah to Steve Cram, along with many others. He knows what he is talking about and he says there is a lot of misinformation out there about running being bad for your knees. If you have nothing wrong with your knees, if you have no pre-existing conditions or injuries, you should have no problems running, he says. 'Alister's research has basically shown everyone that running in itself isn't the bad thing. Most physios now are really keen to get people moving, get them stronger, get them exercising. We know now that making people immobile and sedentary has a hugely negative effect. We know that positive stress is really, really good for bone development and bone tissue. We know that strengthening and being fitter and being lighter is always going to be good for your knees. Everything we stand for in healthcare now is about stopping this fearmongering that running is bad for your knees. We are doing a complete 180-degree turn on it. And we need to start getting away from this horrible language like "wear and tear", which is basically putting people in a chair rather than getting them up and making them active. I think Alister's absolutely right to rename it "inactivity" arthritis.'

I try to remember all their reassuring words as I lie motionless in the MRI scanner. *Clunk, clang, bang* goes the machine. No wonder they gave me earplugs. Finally, the machine stops whirring. The room is quiet. I hear a door opening behind me. Voices. A nurse comes in to extract me from this white tunnel. Next door, indecipherable images of my body are up on several screens. I scan the faces in the room, bracing myself for bad news. Alister is in there, with a few others I do not know. 'So . . . good-looking knees! Pretty perfect, in fact,' says one doctor. I laugh out loud, letting out a huge sigh of relief. 'Really?' I ask, not quite believing them. 'Yup,' says Alister, smiling. 'A pristine knee really. And the cartilage behind your kneecap is looking pretty perfect too. That's where it's really important,' he says, pointing at the screen, 'because seven times your bodyweight goes through your kneecap even when you go upstairs. The force is probably very similar when you're running. Look at it here – it's 7mm thick behind your kneecap but 3mm everywhere else in your body. If there was going to be a vulnerable place, it would be there.' I feel almost giddy with relief. I hadn't realised how stressed I had been getting about these scans. 'Are you surprised by the results?' I ask him. 'No. I'm not now after doing all these studies over the past few years.' 'What about my crisp-bag crunchy knees though? What's that noise all about?' I ask. 'It is called joint crepitus. It's very common,' he says. 'It's basically a vibration because the surfaces under your kneecap aren't smooth and aren't being evenly loaded. It's a misalignment. But I can see from your scans that your cartilage is all right. You must make sure that you keep your muscles strong though. If you look after the muscles, they will look after your joints. That is what we are trying to prove with our scans and research now. From the age of about 30 you lose 1 per cent of muscle a year. But you can change that if you work at it.'

---

I am 54 when I suddenly throw myself down on the floor of a hospital room and try to do press-ups. A nurse walks in, looking confused to see me there, just as my arms give way after managing only one. It's not even a proper press-up, more of a dip. My mother, Jenny, is lying in the hospital bed. At the age of 81, she has gone from being active to completely immobile in the space of two months. She can no longer walk and may not walk much again, according to one of the doctors here.

Watching both of my parents suddenly become frail has been shocking. My mother now has a multitude of problems, from multiple knee replacements and bowel cancer to an untreatable rare brain disorder called normal pressure hydrocephalus that few people had heard of until the singer Billy Joel was diagnosed with it. My father has late-stage Parkinson's disease that has left him increasingly diminished. One moment they were crossing the plains of Africa on horseback and striding out across the cliffs in Devon, now they are mostly confined to their sitting room, hardly moving from in front of the television that is on all day. I fear old age. I run from it. I run many, many miles trying to escape it. But now, watching my mother unable to lift herself up to a sitting position in bed has made me realise that just running is not going to be enough. I need to stay strong. That is why I am lying on the hospital floor, trying to do press-ups and realising that I can't.

My mother was always beautiful, a model turned florist and author who until recently looked at least a decade younger than she was. It frightens me looking at her now that I could, in years to come, become trapped in my body like she is. Mum never exercised like I do. She didn't run, she didn't go on long-distance bike rides. She didn't think that kind of exercise was necessary. But she had a horse, and she rode a lot, going out for hacks a couple of times a week on trails across the Surrey Hills. Occasionally she went for a swim. Her great passion has always been her garden. Which is where she found herself lying just a few years ago, in the flower bed, shouting out for help. She had been wandering around the garden as usual when she bent down to pull up a weed. That's when she toppled over and realised that she couldn't get up. She didn't even have the strength in her upper body to roll over on to all fours. For more than half an hour she was on her back, calling and shouting for help. 'I lay there thinking no one is ever going to find me here. Luckily it wasn't raining,' she laughs. 'It was awful. I did try and get up, but I didn't have the strength; I couldn't move myself.' My father finally heard her. But his Parkinson's meant he wasn't strong enough either to get her back on her feet. He tied his jacket around her and heaved and pulled her but still she wouldn't budge. In the end the neighbours had to be drafted in to help her up.

Four years later Mum is now in a wheelchair, a lot heavier and needing 24-hour care. Her brain disorder affects her balance, her mobility and her personality. It gives her symptoms of Parkinson's and Alzheimer's even though she doesn't have either. She is now waiting for a full knee replacement, after the first one went wrong. Despite being immobile, she is ever optimistic that she will one day be able to walk again. 'I sometimes lie in bed and think I can get up and walk to the door. But then I remember I can't. It's amazing, just amazing to think I used to go out, drive my car, go shopping. It's depressing,' she says, pausing, 'but I'm not depressed.'

---

The knees frighten me of course. I am my mother's daughter after all. My recent scans may be reassuring for now, but they cannot see into the future. And I need to keep moving. Running has given me a whole new identity. It is what I do. It is who I have become, as much a part of me now as my family, my friends, my job. It is my core. It makes me feel solid, young, grounded inside. One foot in front of the other, mile after mile, confidence soaring. *I can. I can. I can.* Possibilities abound. I see others around me slowing down. Yet my early 50s are my fastest years. It is empowering. I feel strong, mentally now, not just physically. It is a deep connection with the earth through the soles of my feet that rebounds back full of energy and strength with every step I take. Alive. In the moment. That's how it feels. I can stay steady, stand tall, keep going, take anything on. I can do all that as long as I can run.

I join a gym. It is full of dumbbells, kettle bells, barbells (think of proper weightlifters with their metal bars and discs on either end and you'll know what I mean). I step into a world of Romanian deadlifts, banded deadlifts, Bulgarian split squats, goblet squats, Nordics, overhead presses, landmine presses, chin-ups, snatches, bent-over rows. This is a foreign language to me. I have to keep asking for a translation.

Ashton Turner is the man who runs the gym and who can decipher it for me. He is in his early 40s, smiley, endlessly enthusiastic and passionate about the business that he set up almost a decade ago. 'Boutique fitness' is what he calls it – small 50-minute classes for up to six men and women, all ages and sizes, though it's targeted mainly at the over-40s. Everyone does the same sessions, just with different weights. 'Your heavy is different to my heavy,' he tells me reassuringly. Though right now I have no idea what my heavy is. We launch into back squats – the barbell balanced on my shoulders as I squat right down to a 90-degree angle. I'm pleased to find my legs are already fairly strong after all the running and so I push more 5kg and 10kg discs on to the bar for each set of eight squats. We rest in between sets. By the fourth round I'm squatting 50kg without too much trouble.

My arms and shoulders though are a mess, which after my hospital attempt at press-ups no longer surprises me. I am put through my paces with pull-ups and chin-ups, hanging from a bar trying to lift my entire bodyweight using my arms and back muscles. It is even harder than it looks.

Dayle is one of the main coaches. He is sandy-haired with a short beard, chunky legs, in his early 30s. He gives off an air of grumpy sergeant major, though there is a discernible teasing twinkle in his eye. He is the only person I know who still tells me off (a lot) for being late, for not listening to instructions, for getting an exercise wrong. He puts us through our paces lifting weights I never thought possible and would never have tried on my own. We deadlift, bending down to pick the weighted bar up off the floor and then stand up straight with the bar just over our knees before putting it slowly back down. It works everything. Your hamstrings, quadriceps, glutes and calves. 'This will not just make you stronger,' says Dayle, 'it'll help prevent you getting injured when you run.'

I start going to the gym three times a week. My body visibly changes and not in the way I expected. People keep warning me I will bulk up. In fact, it is quite the opposite. I am leaner, a different shape to my arms and waist, quads that look more defined already. It feels good and I feel strong. Six weeks after I first walk into the gym, I can feel a difference. I can squat more than 70kg, deadlift 90kg. I can even bang out multiple press-ups now and do one solitary pull-up. There's still work to do but I've lost body fat and gained more muscle mass.

It's the women who surprise me most. Some of them are so unexpectedly strong. One who I get to know is in her 60s. Judith may be older than me but she's stronger and I quickly realise I can't yet lift what she can. I try to keep up with her as she piles on more and more weights. Before I know it, she has lifted 97kg off the ground. I can't even shift the bar when I have a go. 'We have a number of women here deadlifting 100kg,' laughs Ashton, seeing the surprise on my face. 'Some of our women are a lot stronger than our men. It's not a men versus women thing. It's just about consistency. Women train well. They get the results.'

Judith tells me she has had terrible problems with her knee since a skiing accident more than 20 years ago. She had to have a partial knee replacement. But now after a few years' being coached under Dayle's eagle eyes, she has strengthened it so much that she has already climbed up Africa's highest mountain, Kilimanjaro, and is getting ready to trek to Everest Base Camp. 'What I realised with my strength training – and I took it really seriously in the months before Kilimanjaro – was that the more weights I lifted, the stronger I got, and my knee just got better and better and better,' she says.

As the weeks pass, running starts to feel easier. I am not tiring as quickly, even though I have spent less time training in order to make time for my weightlifting. 'Is all this going to make me a faster runner?' I ask Ashton. 'Absolutely! If you don't get a PB in your next marathon, I will sign up for my first,' he fires back and then looks a little worried.

I have bigger matters on my mind right now though, in the shape of mountains. Huge ones. Somehow, I've landed myself in a 35-mile mountain ultramarathon. It's not the distance that's worrying me. It's the three huge mountains in the Alps that I'll have to climb and run down. Right now, I am going to need all the strength in my legs that I can find.

# 9
## *Peak Time*

High up on a narrow mountain path, a couple of miles above a Swiss valley, I decide to overtake one of the runners in front of me. And I fall. The tuft of grass that I put my foot on gives way. I land on one knee. My other leg disappears over the edge. Straight down. There are gasps from the snaking trail of runners behind me. I scramble back on to both feet. My knee is smarting. There's blood. I don't really dare look. Instead, I am forced to keep moving by the long line of restless runners stacking up behind me, all trying to get to the top.

We've been up here for more than five hours already and we're only halfway through this Alpine race. We'd set off from a village in Switzerland early in the morning at the start of the UTMB's OCC, a 56-km (35-mile) ultra run across the Alps, up and over three mountains into France, with more than 3500m (11,000 feet) of climbing along the way. The OCC takes its name from the route that we are running – from Orsières (O) in Switzerland via Champex-Lac (C) in France and then on into Chamonix (C). It is one of the shortest races in the UTMB's world-famous week-long festival of trail running. The main event is the

Ultra-Trail du Mont Blanc – a 170-km (107-mile) journey around Europe's highest mountain that involves more than 10,000m (32,000 feet) of climbing. That's like scaling Everest three times – way too much for me. Though right now I'm beginning to think this 'shorter' version of the race is beyond me too.

It is not easy to train for a mountain marathon when you live in London. My preparation for this race has been far from ideal. I have been working six days a week for months now after taking on Andrew Marr's Sunday morning politics show in January 2022, on top of my usual news bulletin duties on the *Six* and *Ten*. Andrew had suddenly announced he was leaving the BBC, just months into the latest series. I hesitated when I was asked to step into the role, though I knew as I did, that I couldn't really say no. The hour-long political programme at 9 a.m. on a Sunday morning is one of the BBC's flagships. I had already presented it several times about a decade ago when Andrew had had a stroke that stopped him working for nine months. Preparing for it had felt like doing my university finals every week. Intense revision, making sure of my facts before facing the most senior politicians in the studio and interviewing them one after the other live on air. Now I was being asked to do it again, every weekend, until the bosses decided who should take over the role full time. Three months, they said when they asked me, though I knew it would be longer than that. Launching a new programme always takes much more time than you think. I said yes, even though it filled me with fear. I had only just signed up for my mountain marathon. I knew just how much extra effort I would now have to put in for both the Alps and for work.

So within weeks, my normal long Sunday runs were replaced by live interviews with politicians, a marathon of a different kind. My morning would start at 5 a.m. when I would read through as many of the newspapers as I could on my way to work in the back of a taxi before last-minute changes and discussions with the razor-sharp young editor John Neal about new stories that were breaking, or different lines of questioning we should take. The programme was intense. There was no time to breathe as I turned from a cabinet minister to a shadow cabinet minister for 10- or 20-minute-long interviews, trying to gather my thoughts fast and switch effortlessly from one line of questioning to another. It was fascinating and endlessly challenging. I had to concentrate so hard for those 60 minutes that by the time the titles rolled at the end of the programme I felt like I had been flattened by a bus. The idea of pulling on my trainers after that for a three-hour run up Box Hill was far too much. I had no energy left. I just wanted to go home and collapse.

I ploughed on with my training, running to and from work at the BBC in Oxford Circus most days to try and fit it all in before the race in August, taking different routes depending on how far I needed to run. Primrose Hill, north of Regent's Park, is about half a mile away from the newsroom and it was the only place I could find any elevation at all. All 210 feet of it. I would go there and spend an hour or so doing 'hill reps', running as hard as I could up to the summit with its sweeping views across London and then jogging back down, before pushing hard up the hill, over and over again. *It's something at least to get my legs ready for the mountains*, I would think. How wrong I would prove to be.

Trail races are very different to road marathons. Training is much less about the pace of every mile and much more about time on your feet and different terrain. I took to exploring London as a way of distracting myself from the volume of running. One warm and sunny Saturday afternoon, as I was heading home from work, I zigzagged through Hyde Park and its sandy horse trails and then headed out of the gates at Hyde Park Corner and crossed over to Wellington Arch, intending to run through Green Park and on to the Thames Path. I had to weave my way through the crowds, tourists and people strolling through London's parks. A naked man pushing a bike made me stop dead in my tracks. I looked around, completely confused. Why did nobody else seem as surprised as I was to see a naked man casually wheeling a bike through central London? Then there were two. This one was waving, on his bike, heading in the same direction towards the Arch. Three of them now, not a scrap of clothing between them.

I backed away from the path and on to a grassy bank and stood frozen, behind my running sunglasses (mirrored, thankfully), staring as it all unfolded. A handful of bodies turned into hundreds, a steady stream now of naked people and bicycles. Mostly men, with body parts big, small, tiny, shaved, unshaved, dangling uncomfortably at angles from saddles all around me. I stood transfixed and prayed no one would recognise me rooted to the spot, unable to stop staring at the huge variety on public display. Finally, I asked someone, who was wearing clothes, what was going on. I had run into the middle of the 2022 World Naked Bike

Ride, they told me. It was an annual protest against car culture and fossil fuels, plus a celebration of body positivity. I laughed, took some photos and then finally jogged off.

Towards the end of July, MPs left Parliament and went on their summer recess. My seven-month stint on the Sunday politics show was over. Laura Kuenssberg would be relaunching it in the autumn. I was glad to have done it but I wasn't sorry to have come to the end of my time on the programme. It was only once my Sunday mornings had been taken from me that I realised how deeply ingrained in my life long runs at the weekend had become. They were part of its rhythm, a much-needed change of gear. I had missed that time out on the trails.

---

With a month to go before the Alps, I decamped to the Isle of Wight and my godmother's farm near Yarmouth where I have spent a lot of time over the years. The Isle of Wight is 23 miles long and 13 miles wide, almost marathon distance across and a half marathon down. It is a perfect trail runner's island, hilly though not mountainous and very little of it is flat. I bought myself an Ordnance Survey map with all the trails and footpaths marked on it, criss-crossing the fields and coastline of this island off England's south coast. I decided I would try to run as much of it as I could, ticking off each new path with a highlighter pen once it was done. The more I ran, the more my web of routes grew, spreading into a swirling bundle of fluorescent lines swooping in and out of each other on the paper. Each run became an adventure, a new part of the island uncovered.

I ran along footpaths that passed through people's back gardens, through narrow gaps in hedges that I had never noticed before, up long, steep paths under tunnels of trees, the arms of ancient oaks entwined above me shutting out much of the light. My map mission made each run more interesting. I enjoyed the challenge and looked forward to what I might find. This wasn't just training. I was exploring. I would return to the farm each time and mark the latest path off in my godmother's kitchen in front of her husband John, who has lived on the Isle of Wight his entire life. He loved hearing about my latest discoveries. 'You've seen more of this island than I have,' he'd always say with a laugh.

There was one trail that I did run over and over again that summer. My favourite path took me from the farm along the coast towards the small harbour town of Yarmouth, through hamlets with their houses, all facing out to sea. Twisting-turning rutted paths wind through woodland where the water is hidden from view. As the trees thin out, the sea reappears fleetingly through natural windows, small gaps in the foliage, a bench or two to allow walkers to stop and look. At the bottom of a hill is a wooden footbridge over a small creek, surrounded on both sides by tall reeds, bigger than me, that always makes me think of a jungle in the Far East. Out in the Solent, white yachts are in the distance, bright sails billowing, vying for space with the ferries crossing the short stretch of water from Lymington Pier on the mainland. There's no bridge connecting the two. The only way to get here is by boat and it leaves the island comfortingly cocooned, a step away from the rush on the other side of the water. Container ships piled high with cargo and huge cruise liners turn eastwards as they pull out of Southampton. The water throngs with life, unlike the paths I run on. Mostly I have them to myself. In the distance is Yarmouth, one of Britain's smallest towns, with its handful of shops and restaurants, and a square 16th-century castle, built by Henry VIII to ward off the French.

Coastal erosion has left a tree graveyard along this stretch of the path. Enormous, gnarly ancient oaks that have lined this shore for hundreds of years have finally lost their ground and tumbled over into the water. They lie there side by side with their ancestors, blackened by years spent in saltwater graves as the tide ebbs and flows over them.

Beyond Yarmouth is Colwell Bay, marked at one end by a red-brick 19th-century fort, now flats, and at the other end by a trendy upmarket beach-front restaurant, The Hut, to which thousands of people throng every summer. The path drops down on to the beach where I have to dodge families and windbreakers as I run on towards a row of beach huts, their wooden doors painted yellow, red, blue. Along this short stretch of coast, a slice of traditional English seaside mixes in with luxurious motorboats from the mainland which have anchored up here with excited groups of people on board ready for a long rosé-fuelled lunch at The Hut. Their laughter and voices carry across the water. The white shutter-board restaurant is usually packed. Tables piled high with seafood platters; huge magnums of wine being poured into eager glasses. The roof is completely open as the sun pours in, merry diners wearing straw hats with 'Long Lunch' and 'Beach Bums' embroidered in turquoise and red on the front. The temptation to stop, perch at the bar and people-watch is always strong. But that summer I pushed on. The climbs were about to begin and I needed to do a lot more training on steep hills if I had any hope of starting the OCC race in four weeks' time.

One bay along, in Totland, the path along the seafront comes to an end just past the old lifeboat station, and there's a sign pointing up a steep, almost vertical flight of wooden steps. At the top, already breathless, I finally pulled my running poles out of my backpack. They were the ones I had used at the Marathon des Sables and I'd been trying to decide whether or not to use them in the Alps' race. I asked the British ultra runner Elsey Davis, who often races in the mountains, what she thought. 'A lifesaver for your legs, particularly for people who don't have access to mountains for training,' she said. 'Take them! Poles give you four points of contact with the ground, so the load is distributed more. Even if you're saving just a bit of energy with them, that will build up over the race.'

I needed all the energy I could get right now, so I wrapped the straps firmly around my wrists and started trying to propel myself upwards. Headon Warren is where I was going, an open grassy stretch that was cleared of trees thousands of years ago to allow cattle and sheep to graze. Now it is covered in scrubby grass and heather that bathes the cliff side in a purple glow. As I reached the top, trying to keep the poles close to my ankles without tripping over them, one of my favourite views on the island stretched out ahead. The Needles are three huge chalk stacks, 100 feet high, which rise out of the sea like jagged teeth. There's a gap in the line where a fourth stack once stood. It was the highest of the lot, tall and tower-like, a giant needle. It crashed into the sea in the 18th century, disappearing beneath the waves, but the chalk stacks still kept their name. A lighthouse, red-and-white-striped, stands by the last stack, furthest out to sea. Chalk cliffs soar along the southern coast of this island. The Needles mark the point where the Isle of Wight was once joined to the mainland, around 7000 years ago, by a band of chalk that now runs under the sea all the way over to the Dorset coast. From my vantage point, I watched the boats circling The Needles slowly as the gulls and gannets wheeled above them.

The path down to Alum Bay was steep and rocky. I picked my way slowly down and emerged from my solitary run into huge crowds of people. Busloads are brought here to the most south-westerly point of the island to see The Needles and take an incongruous chairlift from The Needles Landmark Attraction Park down on to the beach for the best view of Alum Bay's multicoloured sand cliffs. In the distance, white in the sunshine, across the sea, was Bournemouth. Next to me was a stone memorial that I hadn't noticed until now, despite running through here many times over the years. It marked an unexpected piece of broadcasting history. I was on the very spot where a young 23-year-old Italian inventor and scientist, Guglielmo Marconi, set up the world's first permanent wireless station in 1897. This is where broadcasting began. He and his small team of engineers lived in rooms in what was the Royal Needles Hotel overlooking Alum Bay. They raised a huge mast, more than 150 feet high in the hotel's grounds and worked for months testing their equipment across the open water, communicating first with ships just offshore and then with Bournemouth, 14 miles across the sea. I was standing at the birthplace of radio broadcasting, television, mobile phones, even the internet.

From Alum Bay, I climbed again, 500 feet up on to the chalk cliffs with The Needles now disappearing from view. This is the starting point of the Tennyson Trail, named after the poet, Sir Alfred Tennyson, who also took this part of the island to heart and lived here for 40 years. The chalk cliffs along the island's southern coast stretched out ahead of me as I ran on towards Freshwater Bay. So much here is named after Lord Tennyson, including the vast stone monument that stands at the highest point on the cliffs. The climb to it is steep and once I got to the top, breathing heavily, I forced myself to jog back down and climb it again. Hill repeats for mountain training.

The last stretch into Freshwater Bay was all downhill, a relief after so much climbing, though I would later realise I should have done a lot more downhill running as part of my training. My thighs were about to take a pounding in the Alps. Right now, though, it felt good to fly down the steep hill to the beach. My friend Pip was down there with her big Scottish Deerhound, Mouse, sitting on the wall waiting for me by the water. We swim here year-round. No wetsuits allowed. Normally I screech with shock as I wade into the chilly water. After 14 miles pushing hard on the trails today, I couldn't wait to get in.

---

My last big run on the island was 10 days before my flight to Geneva. A panic run really, as I knew I had not done nearly enough training. My husband dropped me at one end of the island in Bembridge and agreed to collect me much later on the other side at Freshwater Bay. He'd be waiting with food and clean clothes to change into, he said. The run I had plotted was 24 miles in total, from east to west, with more than 3000 feet of climbing. That was just a quarter of the climb that awaited me at the race in the Alps, but it would have to do. The route along the Bembridge Trail was easy to navigate. It was 12.5 miles to Newport in the centre of the island. From there I would pick up the Tennyson Trail, for another 12 miles along the path that would lead me back across the island, down to the southern coast and the beach at Freshwater Bay.

The eastern side of the Isle of Wight is not one I know well but I spent the first few miles scanning the skies for eagles. This is where the white-tailed eagle flies. The UK's biggest bird of prey was wiped out at the end of the 18th century but is now slowly being returned to the island. 'You'll know when you see it,' one of the team behind the reintroduction of the birds told me. 'It's like seeing a flying barn door.'

I ran past Bembridge Windmill, more than 300 years old, the only one left on the island, into countryside once painted by the great landscape artist William Turner. I crossed into Brading Marshes nature reserve with its lagoons and meadows where buzzards, marsh harriers and the eagles soar. A dark shadow out of the corner of my eye made me turn and there high up was a huge bird circling. Only a few dozen eagle chicks have been brought to the island since they were first reintroduced in 2018. Six are taken every year from nests in Scotland, where they are thriving again. They are territorial birds so once grown, the newcomers tend to be chased off by the resident pair. My chance of seeing one was slim, but still the shadow above me made me think I may have been lucky.

I spent a lot of that summer convinced I was going to pull out of the UTMB race at the end of August and stay on the island with my family for the final few days of the summer instead. I have a habit of doing this. Sign up, feel the fear, angst about the race and then try to find a way out. What is it that I'm afraid of? The physical effort? Failing? As ever, pulling out was proving tricky. A great friend of mine, Nuno, a runner from Portugal, who I'd met while he was living in London, was already in Chamonix getting ready to race in the main 107-mile UTMB event. When I called him to express my fears, he just laughed. 'You can't pull out now! That would just be embarrassing,' he said.

---

Orsières is a small Swiss village now swamped with runners. The start line for the OCC is under a blue inflatable arch covered in the UTMB logo. The streets are narrow and we are packed in tightly, bundles of nervous energy, waiting for our race wave to start. There are a lot of us here, 1600 in total. Most of the runners are men. Young, fit, toned. You have to qualify to take part in the UTMB races. Everyone here has run an ultra before. Less than a third of the field are women. Even fewer are women my age. But there is no point in worrying about this now. I have a very long day ahead: 10.5 hours or so, that's what Nuno has suggested. 'You should be able to get round in that time, Soph,' he had told me confidently the night before when I was wolfing down pasta in the hope of extra strength for the race. I have hardly even looked at the route. I haven't even given much thought to the altitude and the extra effort that will involve. The start line is almost 1000 metres above sea level, someone tells me. My mind whirrs. That's about 10 times higher than the highest point I climbed to on the Isle of Wight last week. I laugh. Probably a good thing that I didn't check any of this out.

The first few miles are runnable, but I take it easy. I have been in the Alps for less than 24 hours, no time at all for my body to get used to the altitude. Bright blue skies frame snow-covered peaks. Glaciers tumble down from the mountain tops above us. This is the first time I have seen these mountains in the summer, and they are spectacular. The heat is rising, almost 30°C today. After 5km, the climbing begins and we slow to a steady march. Even the elites have to walk some of the steepest paths. Almost everyone has running poles. Hardly anyone speaks. All you can hear is the *clack clack clack* of poles hitting the ground. The air is thinning. I start breathing hard. My heart rate, visible on my running watch, is climbing fast, too fast, and I am only walking. I try not to panic but those first few miles are nerve-wracking. I have no idea how I am going to cope with this race, this terrain, the altitude.

We pass through small hamlets, cheered on by locals ringing huge Alpine cow-bells. We snake up through the trees along narrow zigzagging paths, strewn with rocks and tree roots – plenty of trip hazards. The valley drops away fast below us. 'Hey! Shouldn't you be reading the news?' someone suddenly shouts at me, a British hiker, who's walking the other way. He stands back to let us pass. 'It would be a lot easier than this!' I gasp, laughing, and keep climbing. It is hard to take in the dramatic scenery when you have to concentrate so hard on your feet. I grab water and handfuls of food as I rush through the checkpoints that pop up every 6 miles. It's important to keep fuelling, eating and drinking regularly as I go, to keep my energy reserves as high as I can.

One water station is a freshly swept-out cattle shed borrowed from the black-horned Swiss cows outside. I can smell the absent inhabitants as I duck in through the low door where there are vats of water lined up on the sloping floor for us to refill our bottles with. I rush out of the water station on to a welcome downward slope before realising I'm missing my poles. I must have left them in the cattle shed. It's a hard run back up to find them.

The altitude starts to get to me on the steepest path up from Trient to Col de Balme, the border between Switzerland and France, more than 2000m (6500 feet) above sea level. It's almost 6 miles of climbing and scrambling up paths, at one point so close to a drop that we are told to hold on to a chain to keep us from falling. A wide torrent of water pours down the mountainside next to us, white crests tumbling over rocks towards the valley below. I feel thirsty. The path twists and turns sharply. There's no summit in sight. Just lines of runners appearing high above us on the mountainside. I start to feel dizzy, light-headed. My legs tingle strangely if I stop. A tall, lean runner near me looks back repeatedly, concerned. 'You sure you're OK?' he keeps asking. Another man stops and is quietly sick behind me. Others sit on rocks in the shade or stand slumped over their running poles. The heat and the altitude are getting to us now. But there's no way out. No help until the next aid station a couple of miles away. So, we press on.

My ears are playing strange tricks in my head. Something has happened to my hearing since we set off. A constant muffling noise in my eardrums, an echo when I speak. It's like being underwater. It's isolating. I've been running in the same pack for a while now. We don't run together but we are never far apart. One man starts talking to me. He talks a lot. A babble of times and stats and percentages climbed, proportions left, targets missed, new targets set, time remaining. Really? That much time?! Questions. Lots of questions. I answer yes, a lot. Yes, you're right. Yes, it hurts. Yes, I've heard you. Yes, I can't speak. Yes, I'm coming. And plod on. He jostles me, cajoles me. We are running together now it seems. He is faster than me, stronger on the climbs, but untrained, he says, not trained enough at least, unsure how long he can go on at pace without breaking. So, we stick together for a while. A balancing act that works somehow.

Nuno has given me rough timings, points that I need to have reached if I am going to get to the finish line within 10 and a half hours. As I climb on upwards towards Col de Balme, the highest point in this race, I keep trying to calculate and recalculate how I am doing because I seem to be so far behind. We are way above the tree line now in a steady march towards what I think is the top. But when I get there, I realise there's still a lot more to go. I arrive, finally, almost two hours later than I thought I would. There's an aid station with copious amounts of food and water. I down as much as I can and try to take in the panoramic 360-degree views of the Chamonix valley. Mont Blanc and the vast glaciers on Switzerland's border before I begin my descent into France.

It's a five-mile run down the mountain now to Le Tour and on into Argentière and then the last big climb of the race. The wide path down looks a lot easier than it feels. The path is steep and twisting. When I finally burst off the trail on to a road and the village of Le Tour in the valley, I hear people wildly shouting my name and turn in surprise. There standing by a water trough is Isobel Lang, who was the weather presenter on BBC *Breakfast News* with me and Jeremy Bowen more than 20 years ago. I stare at her in puzzled disbelief trying to work out why she's there. She's waiting for friends in this race, she shouts to me, before I run on dazed, waving madly at her, throwing water from the trough all over me as I go.

I lose track of time. It gets dusky on our final climb out of Argentière, one more steep path that opens out into what must be a ski run when there's snow here. A ski lift dangles empty overhead. If the climbs are tough, the descents become brutal. It's hours of running downhill, constant pounding, and my thighs are now agony. The final descent through a forest into Chamonix seems interminable. Each step hurts. The lights of the town twinkle. It doesn't look that far away. But it's 4 more miles, someone tells me, and at this pace that's almost another hour. It is dark by now; my head torch is on. I run in its small pool of light, a mesmerising circle lighting up the path. And then suddenly we burst out on to tarmac under street lights and a final climb over a makeshift metal pedestrian bridge, so many painful steps up and then down again, and on into a carnival atmosphere in town and a roaring crowd. Big screens beam live footage of the UTMB races across the week. Cafés are packed with people applauding. I run hard despite the pain.

'Come on, Sophie!' shouts a familiar voice and then I realise it's Nuno. 'There's a man in a giant sombrero on your heels. You can't let someone wearing a hat like that beat you!' But I have no more left. The sombrero sails past. Nuno runs with me through the streets along the final stretch and then ducks out at the last corner with 100m to go. There, finally, is the famous UTMB finish line by the church in the heart of Chamonix. The crowds are packed in on every side, cheering and hammering the barriers with the palms of their hands to make a huge noise. I cross the line red-faced, a huge smile, sweating, exhausted and utterly relieved. It has taken me 11 hours and 54 minutes to get here, a lot longer than I expected. I have been humbled by the mountains. I finish middle of the pack, 12th in my age group. Almost 180 runners have dropped out. There is no medal for our efforts. The UTMB does not do medals. How can I not have a medal after all that? Instead, I am given a baby blue 'OCC Finishers' gilet that I slip on as I am handed a beer. It has never tasted so good.

## 10

## *Harnessing the mind*

The message from the Prime Minister's Director of Communications, Guto Harri, pops up on my phone an hour after I have arrived at the cottage. It's Wednesday and I have a rare three days off on the Isle of Wight. It's my first chance to escape the madness of the past few weeks at work and switch off completely. My happy place, I always think, as I gaze out across the fields down to the sea where the motorboats are cruising and inflatable ribs are going back and forth in search of seals. 'Hi. Fancy the PM this Sunday on your show?' Guto types. *Nooo*, my mind instantly screams. *Not this week! Not now! It's half term. I want time out. I've been looking forward to a few days off so much.* It takes me a full five minutes of staring at his words on my phone before I manage to type back: 'Yes! Of course.' 'Great!' he replies instantly. And I call John Neal, the editor of the Sunday morning politics show, to let him know that the next few days are suddenly going to get very busy.

Another message from Guto the next morning. 'Could you be in Munich on Saturday to do the interview? Might be the only way the schedule works.' The offer is to go out on the Prime Minister's plane, part of the entourage to the Munich security conference. It's February 2022 and Russian forces are massing on the border of Ukraine, though no one is sure if President Putin is really going to order them to invade or if it's just a threat. Whatever his intention, Russia and Ukraine will be the main focus of this conference that world leaders are attending. 'We'll try to find the time for the sit-down interview with the Prime Minister in between bilateral talks,' Guto says. I lean over the fence at the end of the farm garden, looking down at the Solent. This is the only place on the farm where I can get a decent phone signal. I call John and we mull over the pitfalls, what could trip us up. I've only been working on this programme with John and his team for a couple of weeks since Andrew Marr abruptly left at Christmas. This interview is high-stakes. We can't be caught out.

I run. I consider leaving my phone behind, but I can't quite switch off. I head down to the beach where the sea is still flat, despite the fact that one of the most powerful storms for decades, Storm Eunice, is apparently heading this way with hurricane force winds. If I'm going to Munich, I am going to have to get off the island fast. The ferries won't be running when the storm is forecast to hit with gusts of more than 100 miles an hour in two days' time.

Running silences my mind. I rarely listen to music or podcasts or audiobooks. Too much noise in my head already. I need the quiet. I am in the moment. Time stills. Nothing in front, nothing behind. This is the closest I get to meditation, emptying my mind. It is calming. All I can hear is the sea, my feet and my dog Luna, a cavapoo, who barks in excitement as she bounds off ahead of me. The trail is wet, and the mud focuses my attention. I have to concentrate so I don't fall over. As I turn inland, the water is high in the small tributaries that flow into the sea, much higher than I've ever seen it before. The water comes right up to the edge of the duckboards. Even the dog is nervous about her paws as she trots along by my heels now. My phone is on vibrate, just in case John calls with some news.

The long wooden jetty into the creek is broken. Some of the wooden planks have completely disappeared, leaving a gaping hole, which means we can't run out to the end of it as we normally do. The dog is confused and stands staring out at the sea. She knows our normal routine. By the time I get back to the farm with my dog, now muddy and cold, I have 6 miles under my belt and a new footpath that I've run; another one to mark off on my map in my fluorescent green pen. John calls. 'Right, we are on,' he says and I know then that I'm heading back to London already. Less than 24 hours hidden away on the island and I've got to step off before the storm arrives.

We start planning the interview. It's the Prime Minister's first sit-down in six months and a lot has happened since then. The news has been dominated for three months now by the Downing Street parties during the pandemic: 'Partygate' as it has been dubbed. This is the first long-form interview Boris Johnson has agreed to do since the photographs of gatherings during lockdown were initially broadcast. And now there's the threat of war in Ukraine to contend with too. Striking the right balance in my line of questioning is going to be crucial.

The interview is on Saturday afternoon in Munich. We are flying in and out in a day, though not with the Prime Minister's entourage. We decided to get ourselves there. I have to be back in time to be in the studio for the live programme on Sunday morning. I head straight to the office once I am off the island and spend Friday afternoon huddled around a desk with the team working out how we are going to do it. It's a 30-minute interview so it needs to be thought through and carefully structured. There are so many ideas and issues and rabbit holes to avoid. So much information crashing over me, like the winds that are now howling from Storm Eunice outside. Gusts of more than 120 miles an hour have been recorded at The Needles on the Isle of Wight. All the ferries have been cancelled. I was lucky to make it back in time.

Early evening and I run home, to the amazement of John and the team. 'You're about to fly to Germany in the morning to interview the Prime Minister,' he says, 'and you're still running home?' I smile. One foot in front of the other, backpack on. I need to still my mind, to calm it down.

I pack, keep reading my notes and then try to switch off. I've got to be up before 5 a.m. for an early flight. It's the first time I have been on a plane in 18 months, since the pandemic. It's strange to be travelling again. Sleep is difficult. My mind keeps whirring, questions and thoughts turning over in my head. I need to sleep so that I can think straight in the morning, though a lot of sleep isn't looking likely now.

The Covid restrictions in Germany are still tight, much tighter than in the UK. The first thing we have to do when we arrive in Munich city centre is buy FFP2 face masks, a 'filtering facepiece' with a much closer fit than the ones we've been wearing back home. We need these specific masks as well as a vaccine pass and identification just to buy food and coffee. We set up a base in a restaurant by Munich's famous cathedral, the Frauenkirche, with its two towers that dominate the city's skyline and their onion-shaped domes instead of spires. *Zwiebeltürme*, 'onion towers', is the word that rises from a childhood memory. I haven't been to Munich since I was sent on a German exchange to this city at the age of 14.

I can't eat much. Five hours to go and the nerves have a grip on my stomach. John, Hannah, one of the senior producers, and I keep rethinking what we have planned. Information overload. *This is race day*, I tell myself. *I have been here before.* Mind flooded with all the ifs and buts, the things that could go wrong. I start to go quiet, zone in, focus. It is how I prepare for the marathon ahead. A PB effort, this one. The best I can do. I have got to go all out, trust in my training, my preparation, my crew. Approach it in sections. Stop thinking of the whole lot. Pace it. Stay steady on course.

We are filming the interview in the Munich Residenz, the largest city palace in Germany, now a museum. It is a five-minute walk from the Security Conference venue and it is vast, sprawling and spectacularly ornate. There are more than 100 rooms around courtyards, packed with Bavarian history. Our cameras have been set up in one room but we soon realise the marble floors will make the interview sound too echoey, so suddenly there's a mad scramble to find somewhere else in the palace to film in.

A gallery with wooden floors has better acoustics but there are portraits of Jesus all over the walls. We can't interview the Prime Minister with the Messiah on a cross behind him. This last-minute change is unsettling, as if someone is moving the marathon start line just as I arrive.

We find a spot that works at last, by a staircase and a golden-edged door. There's a huge painting, which will be in the shot behind the Prime Minister, though this one is not of Christ. It's a strange place to be doing an interview but time is running out and it will have to do. The chairs are laid out. I sit in mine. I try to get a feel for where I will be, sense the room. The cameras and lights are being rigged up. John and Hannah pull me to one side. 'Are you OK, Sophie? We are worried. You've gone so quiet.' I laugh. It's only now that it is dawning on me just how much I am treating this like a marathon. I am in full race-day mode. I don't think I have ever run a marathon without being quizzed gently by friends about why I'm being so quiet as we are heading to the start line. 'I am totally fine,' I tell them. 'I always do this. I just go quiet. Don't worry. It's all good.'

We head out for some more food, with an hour or so to go. I am thirsty. Hydrate, take on fuel. At a tiny café around the corner, we perch at high coffee tables. I have a double espresso and a soft pretzel that I spot behind the counter. This is what I have done for years now on marathon day. A shot of caffeine and pretzels that the Olympian marathon runner Liz Yelling told me years ago were part of her race-day preparations. 'The carbs and the salt in the pretzels will help you run,' she said. These race-day rituals are soothing.

We 'war game' the interview in the café. My marathon warm-up. Hannah plays Boris. I can barely get a word in. He is verbose and lecturing, never-ending sentences, creating quite a din in this narrow coffee shop. I have to talk over her to ask a question. The next-door table looks round. 'Not too aggressive, don't smile, don't interrupt him too much. He won't be this bad, at least I hope not,' laughs John. The Prime Minister is on the world stage at the Munich security conference. He will want to be statesman-like, calmer than we have seen him lately in Parliament. That may play into my hands. I don't want a fight, even if he doesn't like my questions.

Back at the Munich Residenz near the Frauenkirche, I put on my microphone, plug in my earpiece and take my seat. I am ready. A stream of Downing Street people starts to appear. A delegation including a man in military uniform sweeps by as I sit waiting. Who are they all? More noise now from around a corner. They have to cross a room in front of me to get here, and I have a good view. Voices, footsteps, then photographers walking backwards, snapping away, as the stream turns into a flood of people, flowing towards me, carrying with them a billowing stout figure right in their middle. He's smaller than I remember. Is that just because I'm sitting down?

Boris Johnson takes his royal red chair opposite me. This new space is so tight that our knees are almost touching, which is strange given all the Covid distancing outside. Small puffy white hands. Ruffled shirt, ruffled hair. He laughs as my hairbrush is removed from beside me. 'The last time we met, we flew in a golden plane,' I say. He looks puzzled. It was in Cornwall in 2012 when the Olympic Torch was flown in at the start of the torch relay on its way to London's Olympic stadium. I had been there to do a live interview for the BBC's *One Show* with Princess Anne, Sebastian Coe and David Beckham as they stepped off the plane. Boris Johnson was the Mayor of London back then. 'Oh, the flying custard tart,' laughs the Prime Minister, remembering the specially painted gold plane that they had all arrived in from Athens. It was a flight packed with the famous and powerful. There had been some intense negotiations, as he correctly remembers, about who was seen getting off first. Princess Anne? Sebastian Coe? David Beckham? Boris Johnson? He remembers it all clearly, while he is being micced up for our interview. Royalty had won. I had flown back to London with them all afterwards. *If this plane goes down, it'd be quite a story*, I remember thinking.

Last-minute checks. There is a laugh, an easy charm. 'You must not relax. Don't smile too much before this interview,' my editor John has already said. 'Don't get drawn into that.'

And so, I start. The cameras are recording. I ask my first question. How soon does he think an invasion of Ukraine by Russia could happen? And just like a marathon, I am now underway, settling in. The training pays off quickly. It feels easier than I had thought. It is just me and him. I hold his gaze. I keep very still. Not too much interrupting. He keeps jiggling his foot. I keep it simple, about Ukraine and Russia to start with, his day on the world stage. John is keeping me to time, talking to me every so often through my earpiece. 'You've had nine minutes. Turn the corner now,' he says suddenly. I go straight into the first question about Partygate. This is going to be the tough part. He seems to take a breath, a pause; he knew this was coming. 'I absolutely promise you, Sophie, as soon as I have something more to say about this matter I will do so.' This feels like mile 14 in a marathon. The moment you knuckle down, tell your head to hold firm, tell your legs to run on. So, I go with it, push it, persistent, not rude. I don't give up. 'But if the police find that you have broken the law, broken your own laws that you wrote, will you resign?' I ask. The Prime Minister looks a little pained, then slightly amused, bemused, then tries apologetic. His foot keeps jiggling. I stay with it, keep asking about Downing Street gatherings in different ways, trying to get some answers about what he would do if the Metropolitan Police, now investigating 12 events, found that he had broken the law. He repeatedly tells me there is 'nothing' he can offer me on the matter. This is the 18–20-mile stretch of the marathon, where it's feeling tough and you know there's a way to go. 'But you are being investigated by the police, you've got MPs calling for you to resign, you're living under the constant threat of a no-confidence vote, do you not think you're just burying your head in the sand?' I press on. He stamps his foot and raises his fist, pumping it repeatedly in the air. He has found a spurt of energy here. 'I am fortunate to live in a democracy. I am fortunate to be the Prime Minister of a free, independent, democratic country where people can take that sort of decision, and where I do face that sort of pressure, that's a wonderful thing.' I have pushed through the hard miles, now the finish is in sight. By now he sounds a bit weary. I wrap it all up with a, 'Thank you, Prime Minister.' He jumps up fast to unplug his microphone, leaning in towards me as he does to explain that he really didn't think he could give me an answer to my question on Partygate even though I had asked it in '56 different ways'. 'There is a concern that anything more that I say could add pressure in some way,' he tells me, almost apologetic.

Heads, bodies appear from where they were hidden around the corner during the interview to stay out of sight of the cameras though still able to hear what was being said. The delegation sweeps off in another direction with the Prime Minister again carried along in the flow in the middle. Guto Harri just nods at me as he goes.

John and Hannah are in the room next door, looking a little stunned. We all process what was said. It is hard to judge how it went. Though it felt in the right place. Finally, over the finish line, I sit down in the room full of paintings depicting Jesus on the cross. I feel physically exhausted. 'I want to give you something to celebrate,' John finally says. 'Here! You're still new to this team so I bought you a Diet Coke – it's what the Sunday team all drink.' I laugh. A can of Coke had been my reward at the end of the gruelling long stage in the Marathon des Sables. This one tastes almost as good.

———

It is in Munich that I realise just how much marathon running has taught me to harness my mind. So much of it is a mental battle. When I stand on the finish line at the end of a 26.2-mile race, I watch all the other runners coming in exhausted, emotional, disbelieving that it is finally over.

I know just how hard they have worked to get there. You cannot cut corners. You have to do the training, the hard graft, the preparation. Consistency and discipline are key. There are no short cuts.

Long-distance running has given me enormous confidence too and helped me to stay steady in some of the most stressful moments. A marathon is such a long way. It surprises me every time, and I have run more than 20 of them. Standing on the start line can feel overwhelming. But it has taught me that in life the bigger the challenge, the harder it looks, the more it frightens me, the more I just need to break it down into manageable chunks. Don't think of the whole, think of it in stages. If I have a mountain to climb, at work, at home, in a race, I don't look at the summit. I concentrate on my feet. Small steps will get me there in the end, as long as I keep moving.

It wasn't until the coronavirus pandemic took hold that I realised just how important running is for my mind, my sanity. In February 2020 I went skiing in the French Alps with my husband and children. I came back with a hacking cough, so bad that I had to cut short a couple of London Marathon training runs, which was almost unheard of. But still it didn't occur to me that I might have the virus that was starting to grip the world. China already had thousands of cases a day; Italy's case numbers were also on the rise. 'Don't worry! I've just got a horrible chest infection,' I'd say to my colleagues in the newsroom. 'I haven't been to China or Italy. It can't be the coronavirus.' I had, however, been in a hotel full of French and Italians close to Italy's border. Then Huw Edwards got sick a few weeks later and so did George

Alagiah. Huw ended up in hospital and George was being treated for stage 4 cancer, so both had one of the rare tests available in the early days for Covid-19. And both had it. I have no idea if it was me who gave it to them. But I felt particularly bad about George, whose cancer made him extremely vulnerable. He told me not to feel guilty. 'I think that those of us living with cancer are stronger because we know what it is like to go into something where the outcomes are uncertain,' he said in an interview I did with him on Zoom for the *BBC News at Six* while he was in quarantine at home. As it turned out, he was hardly ill at all, unlike his wife Franny, who struggled with the virus for days.

The upshot of Huw and George both being ill was that I worked all the time. I felt like I was living in the newsroom, often doing the *Six* and *Ten* back-to-back. The first weeks of March were intense. On the Continent, the virus had already taken hold in Italy and was sweeping into Spain and France. It felt like a tsunami was heading our way. We were about two weeks behind in the number of cases and deaths. Every night while I was on TV during the *BBC News at Six*, the latest death tolls across Europe would flash up on the news agency wires on my computer screen in the studio. Often, they made me gasp. From hundreds of cases to thousands in just a few days and the death tolls kept climbing. Spain and France were completely locked down in the middle of March. Spain's lockdown was particularly draconian. No one was allowed to exercise outdoors. No running, no cycling, no walking unless it was for crucial shopping or medicine. *No running? None at all?* I thought, my panic rising, as I delivered this news on TV one night. Those who were caught, even running alone, would be fined hundreds, if not thousands of euros. Was that going to happen here in the UK? Claustrophobia took hold.

On Wednesday 18 March 2020 Boris Johnson addressed the nation on TV and told everyone to avoid all unnecessary gatherings in pubs, clubs, restaurants and theatres and to work from home if they could. Anyone who had a high temperature and a cough should stay at home. The whole household had to stay indoors for 14 days if one person showed signs of symptoms. It was almost impossible to test for the virus at that point. Schools were told to close at the end of the week.

I watched from the newsroom, already gripped by a growing feeling of fear and incomprehension, as the Prime Minister delivered these surreal words. That night after the news, I pulled on my trainers and running backpack and headed out into the darkness. Running had not been banned yet. It was 11 p.m. and I was in Oxford Circus, normally one of the busiest places in the country, with around half a million people in the area every day. I was used to dodging people, weaving in and out of the crowds on the pavement. That night it was deserted. Completely empty. I ran down the middle of Oxford Street, normally jammed with buses and taxis, and I gasped out loud. It was shocking to see this city, that I have spent most of my life in, emptied of people. On and on I ran on my eerie 5-mile journey home. I had no concern at all about being out there alone so late at night. There was no other sign of life except a few buses and taxis and the sound of my trainers hitting the tarmac in the middle of the road.

The nation began panic-buying loo roll. I panic-bought a puppy. We had been thinking of getting a dog for a long time. Our 14-year-old daughter, Georgie, had declared that she couldn't spend her whole childhood without a pet. I offered her a goldfish. She came back with a PowerPoint presentation on why a dog needed to come into our lives. Still, we resisted. Busy lives, unpredictable shifts at work. I couldn't contemplate having a small creature who needed me there all the time. And then came the coronavirus.

With the lockdown waves clearly rolling our way, I turned to Google. 'Cavapoo puppies for sale,' I typed in the week that schools, bars and restaurants were about to be ordered to close. It was 10 in the morning. A photo of a tiny black face with a tufted white chin jumped out from my screen. 'One girl left, ready to go,' said the ad. An hour later my husband, son and I were in the car, driving to Broadstairs in Kent on what turned out to be the last long journey we would take for months. We arrived at a house full of dogs. A mother and father huddled up with their six pups. The smallest was scooped out and handed to us. A tiny, quaking black ball of fluff. We bought her of course, from a man who turned out to be a police officer. I felt somehow reassured despite my reckless puppy purchase. He gave us a discount because of the pandemic. Weeks later, puppies would double in price. We named her Winnie and took her home, waiting in the sitting room for our daughters to come in from school. They were desperately upset that they had to leave their friends and couldn't go to school anymore. And then they saw the tiny black ball of fluff and both burst into tears.

At 8 p.m. on Monday 23 March, the Prime Minister again addressed the nation. I was at home, not working that night. We all gathered round the television in what felt like a wartime scene and listened as this time Boris Johnson, staring straight into the camera, ordered everyone to stay at home. Immediately. We could only go out to shop or for medical reasons. And we could exercise outside once a day. I could run. Thank God I could run. The only people who could go to work were the 'key workers', those who couldn't do their job from home. That was me. I felt a huge wave of relief knowing that I could still go into the newsroom.

I started running to and from work, taking the most direct route possible. I felt guilty spending more time outside than I needed to. For the first few days I copied the NHS workers heading into hospitals wearing their passes to show they had a reason to be on the street. I wore my BBC pass around my neck as I ran, until one day I started hearing stories about NHS workers being mugged for their ID and lanyards. I took mine off and put it in my backpack, which is where it was one lunchtime when I ran alone in the middle of the road along a deserted Piccadilly. It was so extraordinary to see one of London's widest and busiest streets now abandoned that I stopped and started taking photos. Two police officers appeared from Green Park tube station. 'What are you doing?' one of them asked. 'You shouldn't be out here. This is not a time to be taking photos like a tourist,' she said. I explained that I was on my way to work and pulled out my BBC pass. Her expression softened. 'Oh, I know you! You're that newsreader who runs marathons. I'm a runner too,' she said, finally smiling. We had a brief chat about how lucky we were to be allowed outside still, doing what we loved, before they waved me on, with strict instructions to go straight to work. I ran on to Piccadilly Circus with its huge neon billboards. The lights were still on, but who was looking? Giant adverts had been replaced by tributes to NHS workers and the emergency services who were now under huge strain.

The pandemic was the first story I had reported on in more than 25 years at the BBC that I couldn't escape from. I spent all day talking about it at work, writing cues, updating them when the latest shocking death figures flashed up while I was on air. Then at home, like everyone else, it permeated every aspect of my life. There was no escape. It felt suffocating. Being allowed to go outside and run to and from work started to feel like a real privilege. I began documenting what I was seeing in photographs and posting them online, for millions of other people who couldn't see what I was witnessing. During the first week or so I had a constant feeling that I shouldn't be out there running, even though we had been told to avoid public transport if we could. But as the weeks wore on, I became more adventurous with my routes, looping around different parts of the city on my way to and from work. I would always run in at lunchtime, when London is normally packed. Now though the people had gone. They'd been replaced by pigeons looking for scraps. The birds must have been wondering where we all were.

It was the silence that I found most unnerving. A stillness that I had never felt in London before. One afternoon I ran across Hungerford Bridge on the Embankment and dropped down on to the South Bank near the London Eye and the National Theatre. I was stopped in my tracks. 'Oh my God,'

I gasped out loud. No boats on the river, no trains rattling across the bridge to Charing Cross, no planes heading into Heathrow. All I could hear was a flag flapping on a pole and the cry of a solitary seagull circling high above.

I wove my way through Waterloo, Paddington, St Pancras, King's Cross – London's busiest stations through which millions of people normally pour every day. Now there were just a handful of what I assumed were key workers, milling around looking a little lost. Railway staff in high-vis jackets and masks eyed me quizzically, then smiled and waved as I ran past. Harrods, one of the most famous stores in the world, had closed its doors until further notice for the first time in 170 years. Its huge glass window displays of glamorous mannequins had been replaced with giant murals showing NHS rainbows instead.

At the start of April, I ran down The Mall where in three weeks' time I should have been running the 40th London Marathon with tens of thousands of others. I had been training so hard for it that year. I was almost 52 and it was my year of PBs, first in the marathon in Valencia the previous December when I crossed the line in 3 hours 27 minutes and an annoying 1 second, and then in January at the Farnborough Half Marathon where I finished in 1 hour, 34 minutes. I was second in my age group, which meant I qualified to represent England in the over-50s at the international Fleet Half Marathon in March. That too was cancelled. Though at least I still got the England shirt. The Excel centre in London's Docklands, where runners flock every year to collect their London Marathon numbers, was now filled with hospital beds, preparing for thousands of coronavirus patients.

London took on the air of an abandoned film set. A scene from an apocalyptic film. As I ran, my mind would play strange tricks on me, projecting layer after layer of memories, like a kaleidoscope, on the empty scene. My family, my friends, places, parties I had been to, runs that I had done along the banks of the Thames. The city had stopped. It was as if they had all gone for good.

In the end, I found the silence so unnerving that I started talking to myself just to hear a human voice. And then finally I resorted to headphones and listened to the presenter Sarah Montague every day on BBC Radio 4's *World at One* as I headed to work. I needed to hear other people, not just my footsteps and breath.

As lockdown eased, we were all allowed to run more. But overnight, runners had become some sort of pariah. Out there trying to stay fit and healthy in this time of great sickness, runners were suddenly banned from parks and shouted at in the street if we got too close to people who were convinced they'd be covered in the virus as we ran past. Along parts of the River Thames a one-way system was introduced, with council staff in high-vis vests blocking runners' paths. There was a new anger, aggression and fear directed towards people in trainers that I hadn't experienced before.

I will never see London like that again. Thank God. My children will have vague memories of running with me as the lockdowns eased. They may well pass those stories on to their own kids many years down the line. 'I remember when Mum made us run from tube station to tube station along the District Line for a challenge on what should have been London Marathon day,' Ella, my oldest, will say to her brother Ollie, who was 12 at the time. We started at home and stopped at every station all the way to The Mall and Buckingham Palace. We walked a lot, took plenty of photos and by the time we got home we had run almost 12 miles. Far too much for a child of Ollie's age, no doubt. But he insisted on doing a little more to round it up to 13.1 miles. His first half marathon. *That's my boy*, I thought.

Winnie, the cavapoo, was my other running companion. With her short legs and tiny size, I wasn't expecting her to be able to run very far at all, but she soon proved me wrong. I built the distance up slowly from the age of about six months, far too young I now know, but I am so glad I did. Because she wouldn't be with us for long. We ran up on Wimbledon Common, close enough to home but wild enough that I could pretend I was in the middle of nowhere, and Winnie would bound about, jumping branches and chasing squirrels. I had never understood the joy of running with a dog before. In fact, I had never grasped just how much a part of your life a dog becomes. She was the heart of the house when we all needed to be distracted from the roller-coaster stress of lockdowns.

I was interviewed by *Runner's World* magazine about running during the pandemic. Winnie came along to the photoshoot. She charmed them all, bounding along beside me and jumping into my arms on cue. We were to be the cover stars in a couple of months' time. In December Winnie and I joined Susie on the South Downs Way on Winnie's longest run yet. She was almost a year old. It was joyous. This tiny bundle of curls springing along in front of us for 7 miles. She didn't seem tired at all. It was a new kind of companionship that I wasn't used to, a deeply fulfilling discovery.

A day after *Runner's World* was published, starring Winnie and me, I was doing both the *Six* and *Ten*. It was a cold, dark Friday evening in December, and I ventured out after the first bulletin to find some food. I was heading back to work when my mobile phone rang. It was our nanny, Mimi, her voice desperate, urgent: 'Sophie, what is the vet's number? I need to know now. Now!' 'Why?' I asked, already feeling a dark sense of foreboding. 'Just give me the number; Richard will call you.' I sent it to her and stood frozen to the spot by a post box. My phone rang again. This time it was Richard. He could hardly speak. 'I am so so sorry, Soph. Winnie has been hit by a car. She got out. I don't know how. We tried everything. But she's dead,' he almost whispered, his voice cracking.

I let out a wail in the middle of the street and began to sob. My dog, dead? How could she be dead? She had been curled up on my lap just a few hours earlier. I stood there in the middle of central London crying, my shoulders heaving. People bustled past me, a family with two kids glanced over, but no one stopped. Not one person asked if I was all right. I called the newsroom. They couldn't work out who the distraught woman on the phone was. 'It's me, it's Sophie,' I had to repeat over and over again to my editor, Lizzi. 'My dog is dead.' She sent me home. I couldn't speak. They had to track down my colleague, Jane Hill, and get her into work fast for that night's 10 o'clock bulletin. She only just got there in time.

Our middle daughter was at a birthday dinner a few miles away. I called Georgie. 'I've got to pick you up. Something has happened to Winnie. We need to get home,' I said, trying not to cry on the phone. 'Mum? What? She's not dead is she? Winnie's not dead, Mum? Promise me that?' I scooped Georgie up in a black cab and confirmed what she had already guessed. I had to explain to the cab driver that our dog had died because by now we were both in floods of tears.

At home, everyone was there, except Ollie, who was still at his football practice. In the kitchen, there was Winnie, lying on a towel on the sofa. She looked like she was asleep. I fell to my knees and screamed. A loud, raw scream that I have never uttered before and never uttered since. No one could understand how she had got out that night. Winnie, for all her running prowess and affection, had one fatal flaw: she was obsessed with chasing squirrels, and the wheels of bicycles and cars. She knew where the local squirrels lived at the end of the road and that night, the door must have been left ajar and she ran out.

No one realised she had gone until Mimi was leaving for home and saw a girl crouching in the middle of the road. She thought the girl had been hit but then realised she was leaning over a dark bundle of curls. Richard and Ella ran out. They carried our dog to the front doorstep and even tried mouth-to-mouth resuscitation, desperate for her to survive. But it was too late. She was dead.

Weeks later, when I tracked down the young girl who had found her, she told me what had happened, how she had seen her lying there, still alive, just. The car hadn't stopped. 'I was kneeling with her, holding her paw, saying you were on your way. She looked at me, I stroked her and looked for a phone number on her collar. Then she sighed and closed her eyes. She was in no distress, just a patient, beautiful dog accepting it was time to go. I'm so sorry.'

I had never understood the grief that comes with losing a dog. I had friends who had lost dogs over the years. When they died, I couldn't quite understand why they were so devastated. They had lost a pet. Sad, but they'd move on and get another one maybe. Now I understood the full force of sorrow that came with losing an animal. Winnie had been so central to our lives during the past year of the pandemic, lockdowns, some of the most difficult times. I cried every single day for two weeks. My Belgian neighbour, Marie, saw me in the street one day. She had heard what had happened. '*Winnie était une étoile filante,*' she said to me in French. A shooting star who came briefly into our lives, brought light and then disappeared.

Two days later, Susie, Shaun and some of my Marathon des Sables gang forced me to go and run with them. We went to the North Downs Way near Guildford and took the steepest, narrowest route up to the top of St Martha's hill, a path with steep banks on both sides. 'This way up is known as "Martha's Crack" around here,' Susie told me smiling as they tried to cheer me up. I hung at the back, next to Shaun – 'the Rock', as I had dubbed him in the Sahara. Shaun is a man who is utterly obsessed by his three dogs. I knew he understood. Being out with my running friends was a good tonic. These were people who had seen me in the desert at my lowest point and I didn't have to hide anything now.

'Tell me this is going to get easier, Shaun,' I kept saying. 'It will get easier,' he said quietly, 'but not for a while. You will find another dog who you will love just as much, but differently,' he promised. I didn't believe him, much as I wanted to. My dog had gone. But I still had these precious friends, who threw a circle around me and carried me along that day on a 10-mile journey across the hills.

# 11

## *More than just a run in the park*

The hearse pulls up in front of the church on Kew Green by the Thames on the outskirts of London. It's a beautifully crisp, sunny, autumnal day, the perfect kind of day for a run. A long line of people is queuing to go into St Anne's. In front of me, in among the well-dressed mourners, I glimpse a man wearing his 'parkrun 100' jacket and trainers. I know I am in the right place. This is my first parkrun funeral. The church is packed. We all file past a huge photograph of Serge Lourie, beaming back at us. He was 78 when he set off with a group of running friends on his usual 5k from Kew to Chiswick Bridge and back along the River Thames. Afterwards, as always, they went to a local café for coffee and croissants. Then Serge went home, lay down on the sofa and died. It was a poetic way to go for a man who was passionate about running but a huge shock for his family and friends. We all just thought he would go on and on and on.

Serge was a parkrun fanatic. He was almost 60 when he ran his first in a decent time of 29 minutes and 37 seconds. That was 2007 when Richmond parkrun was only two months old. For the next 17 years Serge was an almost-guaranteed fixture at the Richmond Park start line every Saturday morning at 9 a.m. If he wasn't running, he was volunteering, helping organise the timed 5k race for the hundreds of people who turn up every week. His parkrun statistics say it all. By the time Serge died, he had run 473 parkruns and volunteered 207 times. Serge first pulled on his trainers in the 1970s when he was coaxed out of the door by one of his neighbours in Kew. His maiden run was the exact same 5km stretch of the Thames that he ran on his very last day.

Serge loved to talk to people, which is how I first met him when I turned up alone in 2011 for my own inaugural parkrun. He bounded up to me, a great welcoming smile. 'You're that newsreader,' he boomed. 'Meet my friend, Sally Woodward Gentle. She works in TV too!' And that is how many years of Sunday morning runs with Serge, Sally, Mike and the Kew runners began. Sally didn't just work in TV as it turned out; she was one of Britain's most successful drama producers. She was the woman who picked up the ebook novellas by Luke Jennings called *Codename Villanelle* and turned them into the global TV hit, *Killing Eve*. It took me a long time to discover this because every time we all met up, none of us ever wanted to talk about work. Running was our escape.

We would meet in the road where Serge lived at 8 a.m. Half the street would turn out to run. A gaggle of all ages, paces, shapes and sizes, we'd head up to Richmond Park for at least 10km before running back to Kew again for coffee and croissants at Sally's. Serge, Sally, Mike and co. were the first to teach me that running is not lonely. Far from it, in fact. When I set out with them, I had no idea of the deep running friendships ahead, the lifelong bonds that I would make along the way. Running is such a levelling sport. That's what they quickly taught me. It took me ages to discover what any of them actually did when they weren't dressed in Lycra. Serge, as I eventually found out had been a prominent local politician, a Liberal Democrat, the leader of Richmond council. The church was packed on the day of his funeral. Even the former Lib Dem leader, Vince Cable, was there.

It was the absence of Lycra that confused me. It took me a while to recognise people. I rarely saw my friends out of their running kit, let alone in sombre attire. I found Sally and squeezed in next to her and her husband and daughter and then scanned the faces for other people I knew. Women with blow-dried hair and make-up on, men in suits and ties. I had to study their faces for a few extra seconds than normal just to make sure. Others were much easier to spot. When I glanced down at the rows of feet packed into the pews, I smiled because so many were wearing their running shoes in a touching final farewell to our parkrun friend.

It was my first running coach, Karen Weir, who introduced me to parkrun just months after I ran my disastrous debut marathon in 2011. Karen is one of the 'parkrun pioneers', one of the original 13 friends who were lured to Bushy Park in South West London in 2004 by Paul Sinton-Hewitt. Paul, a keen runner, was injured, depressed and had just lost his job. He was missing his running friends, so he gathered some of them together with the promise of a timed run at 9 a.m. every Saturday followed by coffee and a chat. What none of them knew on their maiden run that October was that they were starting a running movement that would sweep the globe and transform the lives of millions of people.

Bushy Park Time Trial, as it was originally called, was small and it was completely free. Thirteen people ran the first one, 14 turned up the week after. Numbers dropped a little on the third weekend. A month after it started there were 20 runners racing each other for the finish line. Paul kept a meticulous record of all their times using small metal discs that he had made up with numbers stamped on each one. As each runner crossed the line, a volunteer would log their time with a stopwatch and hand them a numbered disc telling them which position they'd finished in. It took six months before the number of runners reached 50 and a full year before it hit 100. And that is when parkrun really started to take off.

As word spread and numbers swelled, Paul and some of his friends launched other parkruns nearby. The next was on Wimbledon Common in 2007, followed just months later by Banstead Woods in Surrey and then Richmond Park. Karen Weir was put in charge at Richmond. 'You were given a laptop by Paul and a set of the metal tokens. People had to register by Friday lunchtime if they wanted to run,' she says. 'On Saturday morning we'd bring a picnic table and a chair and often an umbrella to stop the laptop getting soaked. There was so much kit,' she laughs. 'And I'd sit there come rain or shine and runners would cross the line, give me their token with their finish number and we'd put it straight into the computer database. We had about 50 or so runners every week. It got complicated when people had common names. If someone came up to me and said, "Hi, I'm Andrew Brown," we'd say, "Well which Andrew

Brown are you?" So, people had to give us a catchphrase or another name. One of our original Richmond runners is known as "Andrew Kew Brown", because that is where he lives. That way we always knew it was him.'

Nowadays there are more than 800 parkruns taking place every Saturday at 9 a.m. in parks all over the UK and more than 2000 around the globe. It's free to sign up, it's free to run, jog or walk. You don't have to tell them you're coming any more. You just turn up. Its ethos is all about being accessible to everyone. Its name, parkrun, is never written with a capital p, just to underline that point. The metal discs for timing are long gone. Instead, you have your own unique barcode that is scanned after you cross the finish line at whichever parkrun you choose to go to that week. Your results are logged online.

---

Stags with huge antlers stand half hidden in bracken, sheltered by trees, chewing slowly, watching on, as hundreds of people head to the start line at Richmond parkrun. I scan the faces looking for my friends. Young and old, parents with babies in running buggies, dogs straining at the lead, small children in their parkrun T-shirts who don't look big enough to be running 5km. Old women, young women, teenagers, people who look like they have had to haul themselves out of bed a little hungover. Every shape, size, age, fitness and form. If running were a religion, parkrun would be its church. By 9 a.m. on a Saturday morning, we, its congregation, are all gathered right here.

I dip under the tape into the starting funnel to find a place about a quarter of the way back from the front of the pack. It may be a run, not a race, but I am competing against myself, as always. After a few weeks of extra speed training, I want to see if any of it has paid off. We are packed tightly together, bouncing around to keep our muscles warm as the volunteers begin the countdown. The first few hundred metres are uphill. It's muddy and there are tree roots, so I have to pick my way along the path, trying to get some grip and not fall over. On the crest of the hill, the path, now tarmac, levels out and I settle into my pace, listening to the heavy breathing and the rhythmic sound of feet pounding the ground all around me.

Up ahead, I spot Jeremy, a long-time parkrun friend – same age, same pace – who should finish in roughly the same time. My competitive streak fires up as I push on to try to catch him. We are flying down the big hill now, Canary Wharf, the London Eye, the BT Tower, London's skyline miles away but in full view. I'm running fast, my feet turning over at speed. I pass Jeremy. I glance at my watch: 7-minute mile pace, I'm on track for a good time. Jeremy and I play cat and mouse as we turn towards Sheen Gate. We don't speak but we are both now signed up to this chase. 'Thank you, marshal,' people shout out to the volunteer standing on her own, pointing us all in the right direction. I try to thank her too but am struggling for breath. Jeremy is on my tail now. I can see him as I glance over my shoulder when the path bends again and the climb starts. It's not that steep at first, but it grinds away at you, a gentle upward slope before the final big hill. I dig in, trying to break it down in my head, focusing on what is now, not what will soon be.

Running alongside so many others lifts me and drives me on, making me run faster than I would if I were alone here. A mile to go and I am overtaken by a small child. 'How old are you?' I manage to gasp, laughing. 'Ten,' he shouts back before surging ahead with his proud father. The last hill requires distraction techniques. I look for deer, I look for friends, I look for Jeremy, still behind me I think, and I try to pick off a runner or two up ahead. Anything to keep my legs moving because my muscles are now screaming. At the top, I see Bill Neely, a wiry, fit TV journalist I've known for years. He is so speedy that he has already finished and run back to clap us all in. Then the final dash, 200m to the end. The small kid is just ahead of me. I can't catch him. It's a full-on sprint now because Jeremy is on my heels. 'Go Sophie,' people start shouting as I throw myself at the finish line, just seconds ahead of him. A volunteer, in charge of time-keeping, registers our positions as we cross the line. I stumble gasping into the finish funnel. I've come in just under 22 minutes, my fastest run on this hilly course for a while. 'I'll get you back next week,' Jeremy laughs. And I know he will.

At Richmond parkrun I discover a tight-knit community that I had no idea existed within London's vast, sprawling city, a new tribe, a gang of people I connect with, who make me feel instantly at ease. No one judges me, no one tells me I should be faster or fitter. I can go there and race myself, or race my friends, or jog it slowly, walk it even. There is always a volunteer at the very back so no one else is last.

This is what I tell my friend Steph over and over again when she point-blank refuses to come with me. We had met years ago through our children who were at nursery school together. An Australian living in London with four young kids, she had piled on a lot of weight after a few traumatic years. She had lost her first babies, twins, when she was more than five months' pregnant. She got pregnant again and suffered for years with terrible postnatal depression. She started drinking and her depression got worse. By now she weighed at least 80kg. 'In the end I had an almost total breakdown when my fourth child was just eight months old,' she tells me years later. 'I just got to the point where I was standing on the side of the road, thinking, *If I wasn't going to be alive anymore, would it be the 220 or the 430 bus?* I wasn't suicidal but the fact that I was thinking that really freaked me out. So, I stopped drinking, I started walking, then running a bit. I lost around 20kg. And then you dragged me to parkrun,' she says. 'I was scared shitless.'

It took me a full six months to convince Steph to come and run with me. She had started running on a treadmill so that no one would see her. But then slowly she began venturing out on her own along the river, running and walking between lamp posts on the Thames Path. 'I ran past three lamp posts without stopping,' she'd tell me triumphantly. But the idea of running with other people horrified her. She was still heavier than she wanted to be, and she was sure people would judge her. I insisted over and over again that parkrun wasn't like that and that she would feel nothing but supported, but she couldn't and wouldn't believe me. Then finally, after months of pestering, she gave in.

I made sure we got to Richmond Park with plenty of time to spare. She was so nervous that I was certain she would back out, but she arrived, clutching her barcode, with her husband Rob and the children, and I kept her busy, introducing her to all my running friends.

'I was just so scared of the unknown, scared I wouldn't be able to run that far all in one go. You feel like you're not going to be good enough, even though people always tell you that parkrun is all-inclusive. If you haven't experienced it, it just seems too good to be true. But it is true. There isn't any judgement,' she says.

I didn't run with her that day. *Too much pressure,* I thought. But once I got to the finish line, I doubled back and ran to find her in the last few hundred metres of her first timed run. One of her kids came with me and we ran alongside her, cheering and whooping as she got to the finish line in 30 minutes, 30 seconds. 'You were so excited for me,' she laughs now. 'You'd hardly even caught your breath and you were saying, "You see! You can do it! You ran 5km without stopping! Next time, 10km!"' Which is exactly what she did. Now in her early 50s, Steph has run 17 marathons and two ultras, including the TransRockies in Colorado, a six-day race over 120 miles with more than 20,000 feet of climbing.

'I owe parkrun so much,' she says. 'I didn't realise how much I needed it back then. It has been amazing. I can't imagine my life without running now. It was my little midlife crisis. It was the biggest pivot point in my life – of all the things we've done as a family, more than any international move, going to parkrun that day and learning how to run was the most life-changing thing for me.'

More than a decade after her parkrun debut, Steph and her family are living in California, where she has helped set up her own local parkrun in Byxbee, Palo Alto. It is the only one in the whole of California, where there are around 40 million people.

---

My best time ever at parkrun is 20 minutes and 31 seconds. That was just weeks after I had returned from the Sahara Desert, almost a stone lighter. Race weight, I think they'd call that. I was 50 by then and I remember feeling so light, as if I were flying. For months afterwards, I tried to beat that time. I got close but never quite made it. Now in my late 50s, age and parkrun are becoming intricately bound in my head, which is not a particularly good thing. Five kilometres is no distance at all when you are a marathon runner. But 5km at full pelt is no less painful than a marathon at a good pace. It's just over much faster. The margins are so tight that if you slip off pace for even 30 seconds, you are unlikely to make up the time. Increasingly I am finding myself in a weekly battle with my head, legs, heart and body as I try to prove that age is not finally slowing me down.

The man I blame for all this (somewhat unfairly) is a personal trainer and friend called Graeme Hilditch. When I was 45, I started complaining to him about how hard I was finding it to get faster. 'Well, Sophie, you're in your mid-40s now, aren't you? You're probably hitting your physiological peak,' he said. My eyes widened, my jaw dropped. My physiological what? 'It happens to us all at some point,' he said, trying to reassure me. From the look on his face I could see he realised he'd hit a raw nerve. 'We age, we slow down. That's just what happens. That's life.'

## MORE THAN JUST A RUN IN THE PARK

What running has taught me without a doubt is that I thrive on a challenge. If someone tells me I can't, I am instantly fired up to show them that I can. And so poor Graeme (who I know meant well) has had to suffer years of me proving to him and to myself that I can and will get faster.

Jacquie Millet is the woman I always turn to when I worry about the impact of ageing on my running. I remind myself constantly that I am roughly the same age as she was when she bought her first pair of running shoes at 57. A cancer scare prompted a doctor to encourage her to exercise. She started by walking more but was quickly bored, so broke into a jog. 'I found I enjoyed it,' she says, 'but I wasn't very sure what I was doing with it. I'd try to run a little faster when I went out, but it all seemed a little aimless. There was no way I was going to join a running club. I thought that was for proper runners. I was clueless really about the whole running world.' Then she heard about Richmond parkrun and decided to go along.

'I think I might have stopped running if it hadn't been for parkrun. It really motivated me; the people really motivated me. I got so much positive feedback from people. Starting as an older runner, I really didn't know if there was a place for me in the running world. I felt a bit of a fraud trying to be a runner but parkrun really legitimised it all and it gave me a sense of purpose.'

A small, dark-haired, determined woman, it was Jacquie who had dragged me over the last few miles of the Boston Marathon when she was 61. By then she had already run 44 marathons in less than four years. Now at the age of 72, she has clocked up 235 marathons and 20 ultras, including the famous 55-mile Comrades Marathon in South Africa, which she has run eight times. And she's still going.

'What drove you to run like that?' I ask her.

'I think it was because I started so late. Suddenly there was this whole world of exciting events, and I wanted to do as many of them as I could. I thought I'd probably left it too late but decided to give it my best shot. I figured I had about five years of running after my first marathon just before I turned 60. As it happens, I didn't need to be in such a rush.'

I tell Jacquie that I'm wondering if I've hit my peak, if I'm slowing down. 'Really? I don't think you have,' she says, in her cool and measured way. 'I would give it another go. I'd try for another PB, if I were you.'

Which is exactly what I do. With disastrous consequences.

# 12

## *Stopped in my tracks*

I am flying through Canary Wharf, past screaming crowds. The noise is intense, deafening, almost too much. People stand 10 deep along the course, signs aloft, necks craning to spot friends and family in the endless stream of feet. I've trained so hard for the 2024 London Marathon, months and months of runs and races leading up to this one day. It is April and I am just weeks from my 56th birthday, determined to prove that age does not need to stop me running fast. I know that I can finish this race in well under 3 hours, 30 minutes. If I keep pushing like this, I should get a PB. Every time my mind falters and starts telling my body to slow down, I give myself a sharp reminder that if I hold my nerve and keep this pace going for just one more hour, I won't ever have to push this hard again.

Someone starts shouting behind me. I don't hear what he says. Too much noise. Too tired now to make sense of what's being said. Suddenly a sharp shove in my ribs as a man elbows me aside. 'Hey, don't push me!' I shout furiously, amazed that I can still string a sentence together. 'Get out of the way,' yells an American voice. 'Blind runner coming through – why the hell don't you move?' I am stunned by his aggression. 'I didn't hear you,' I shout back, furiously. 'So bloody rude, we are all knackered too,' gasps a woman next to me, as the American and the blind runner sail on past.

I don't know if it is the tight twists and turns of the roads in Canary Wharf or the hard shove from the American, but this is the moment when my ankle suddenly gives way beneath me. My pace slows instantly. My left leg is taken over by shooting pains and starts shutting down. My right leg is trying to power on. It doesn't seem to have got the message yet that we are slowing down. I hobble, limp, lurch for almost 2 miles, swallowing paracetamol, as I try to find my pace again. My mind runs over the injury problems I've endured in the last two London Marathons. A sore calf that brought me up short for a while but that I somehow managed to run through. Can I do that again now?

I start walking at a water station on a bend in Canary Wharf and hear someone shouting my name. My friend Magnus from work is flying past waving at me. 'Are you OK? Do you need painkillers?' he yells over runners' heads. I point at my foot. Then a strange sight as he turns and runs back towards me, against the flow, to try to help. It's the kindest gesture from a colleague who I know is chasing his own PB today. I wave him on and tell him not to worry. I've already swallowed as many painkillers as I can. He frowns, waves again and then he's gone, and I stagger onwards wondering if I am going to have to walk to the end. I can hardly put my foot down now. This pain is too much. It will be a very long walk.

On the side of the street as the crowds thin out near the 20-mile marker, I see a friend, and step off the marathon course on to the pavement and stop. Bob and I have run many races together. He's 10 years older than I am but just as fast. He should be running today but he is out with injury after being forced to pull out of a race a few months ago. 'What do I do?' I ask him over and over again. 'Do I just try to keep going? Shall I walk to the end?' All those thoughts of running down The Mall in record time have evaporated, gone. Bob tells me to try jogging up and down the pavement to see how it feels. I take three steps and straight away more shooting pains up my left leg. 'Just stop,' he says. 'You will make it so much worse if you push on now.' I stand there bewildered.

It turns out that I have stopped in a good place. There's a St John Ambulance medical tent on the other side of the road. I haven't visited one of those since my marathon debut 13 years ago. Back then I was stretchered in unconscious. This time I arrive hopping after Bob manages to manoeuvre me across the road with me shouting 'sorry, sorry' to the tired runners trying to dodge me as I cross their path.

There are two young physios there who sit me down on a stretcher and poke around at my foot. I am smiling and laughing, stupidly cheerful, trying to hide the crashing disappointment inside. *All that training,* I keep thinking, *all that effort and hard work.* There's no swelling, no sign of bruising. My ankle doesn't hurt when they touch it. So, they strap it up tightly and then urge me to go on if I want to. 'It's only 6 more miles. You're almost there,' says one as I try to walk again. More shooting pain. Bob looks a little wide-eyed at them, then at me. I know what he's thinking. 'How bad's the pain out of 10?' the other physio asks. 'Eight, maybe nine,' I wince. The looks on their faces change. 'Really? That bad? You don't think you can get to the end on it?' This is my 12th London Marathon, not my first. How much do I want that medal? Enough to begin a two-hour walk? My mind is whirring with so many questions and calculations. And then suddenly I just give up. It's over. My first marathon DNF – Did Not Finish. I don't need to make whatever I have done to my ankle any worse.

Bob gives me his coat. He insists that I take it. He has fresh memories of a freezing 6-mile limp back to the start line at the half marathon in Cambridge last month when he also had to pull up in the middle of a race. He's not going to let me shiver with cold like he did. There's a Docklands Light Railway station nearby. With the help of one of the medics, we have to dodge the runners once again to get back across the road. I lean on Bob's shoulder and hop and limp and shuffle towards Poplar station. Bob makes sure I get on to a train before he disappears back into the crowd to continue cheering on friends. Now I have to work out how to get to The Mall and the marathon finish line because that's where all my belongings are, including my phone, on the back of the baggage truck that was loaded up at the start.

At Canary Wharf a young girl appears beside me and offers me her shoulder. 'Put all your weight on me, it's fine,' she says to me, a complete stranger. We laugh as we hobble through the station and on to the escalator. She manoeuvres me on to the tube and runs out again. She's travelling in the other direction. For once, I don't hesitate when someone offers me their seat and I collapse heavily into it. The carriage is packed full of marathon spectators on an underground chase popping up at various locations along the course. People are tracking their friends on mobiles. They're confused to find a runner sitting beside them. 'Aren't you that newsreader?' one asks me. And then the heads begin to turn. Sympathy and chocolate eggs and Jelly Babies are thrust at me. And we all laugh about the odd situation I'm now in.

It's another long hop from Green Park to The Mall, leaning on the shoulders of more kind strangers. The finish line is full of its usual marathon day exhaustion and joy. Relief all over the faces of thousands of people as they stream under the gantry and stop at last. I've felt that huge smiling relief so many times before. Now I'm here, on the wrong side of it, being congratulated yet again and having to explain repeatedly that I had to drop out miles back. There'll be no medal for me. I'm just here for my bag. Richard Whitehead, the Paralympian on two blades, is in the VIP area, ecstatic after finishing the whole race in a world record time of 2 hours, 41 minutes. I sway next to him on one leg. 'A photo of you both?' a photographer asks, and I find myself, arm around him, leaning a little too much. He staggers back. I'm already off balance. The man on the blades with the new shiny world record is almost felled in the VIP tent on to a red carpet by the limping newsreader whose ankle hurts. I realise what's happening just in time and lurch forwards. We both remain standing, just, at the finish line.

---

An X-ray and an MRI scan reveal that stopping at mile 20 was the right thing to do. I limp into the consultant's office expecting to be told that I've done some damage to a ligament or tendon, something that will be fixed soon enough. He pulls the scans up on to his computer. My ankle looks like a black-and-white jigsaw puzzle, big bits, smaller chunks, dark in the middle and outlined in white. Except for two of the chunks, one quite big, which is swirling white, cloud-like inside. 'That should be black like the rest of your bones,' he says. 'You have something called oedema of the talus, a rare injury in a runner. This is more the sort of thing you see with snowboarders.' The bone he is pointing at is at the bottom of the bones in my leg, the tibia and fibula, where the leg meets the ankle. 'Your talus is not actually broken,' he says, 'but the bone has been stressed; it has been loaded too much. It is bruised inside.' And then he looks at me sternly. 'You must take this injury seriously. If you're not careful it could fracture. The talus bone has a poor blood supply so it can take a lot longer to mend. And if it doesn't mend, you're also at risk of talar necrosis.' I have no idea what that means. But I do remember from O-level Latin that *necrosis* means 'death'. That doesn't sound good. 'If that bone loses its blood supply it will begin to die. And then you could be in all kinds of trouble. You really must respect this injury,' he says again. I won't be running for a while then. That much is clear. 'I can cycle though, can't I?' I ask hopefully. 'No! No exercise at all. Nothing that will put too much load on your ankle right now. I'd prefer you not to be walking much either, if you can help it,' he says. 'Swimming's OK?' I ask, aghast. 'Only if you don't use your legs,' he says. I leave in a daze. 'How about Kayaking?' suggests a friend.

I feel flattened. It has been years since I was last injured and forced to rest. Running and exercise are engrained in my life. I start mentally deleting the races I've booked – a mountain ultra, an Isle of Wight half marathon. It feels devastating given how hard I have worked over the last few months. I call my friend Rose Harvey, a lawyer who lost her job during lockdown and who, like so many others, turned to running during the pandemic. Rose was already a good runner with a 3-hour marathon to her name. But she quickly discovered she was a lot better than that. Now, three years later, she has just been selected to run for Team GB at the Paris Olympics in the summer. And Rose knows all about dealing with injury. She was out completely for three months last year after being hit by a car that pulled out of a driveway as she was running past on the pavement. She ran into the side of it and landed on the bonnet, hitting her knee hard.

'How on earth do you deal with not being able to run when for you there's so much at stake?' I ask. 'Injury is really mentally tough,' she says. 'Not being able to do what you love and suddenly your love for running becomes even greater when you can't do it. But rehab and recovery are a really important part of training. If you do it properly and don't rush it, you can come back even better, even stronger than before. You'll be back before you know it,' she says. 'Enjoy yourself! Use the time to do the things you can't do when you're training hard. Most injuries are just a lack of strength somewhere, a bit of an imbalance. Get ready to strip it all back, strengthen what wasn't strong enough, and you'll be off again.'

I try to stop and give in to it. I have long lie-ins on Sunday mornings. I rest. It's a struggle. I do what I'm told, mostly.

The call comes six weeks later as I am finishing breakfast at the Hôtel de la Plage in the town of Courseulles-sur-Mer in Normandy. It's June 5th, the eve of the 80th anniversary of the D-Day invasion. The coastline is thronging with visitors from all over the world, here to mark the moment in 1944 when the liberation of Nazi-occupied France finally began. The roads are busy with military enthusiasts, people dressed up as World War Two soldiers, driving in vintage jeeps along the beaches where so many teenagers and young men came ashore under machine-gun and canon fire almost a century ago.

'What have you been doing?' says the voice in my phone. 'Please tell me clearly. Your scan shows it has got worse, not better.' The voice is my consultant's and he is calling me five days after I had another MRI to see how well my injured ankle is recovering. It has been feeling OK, a little stiff at times when I walk. But I had been expecting his call to tell me that I'm on the mend and can think about running again. 'Did you do as I said? Did you limit your walking? Did you take it easy?' he goes on. Now is probably not the time to tell him that my ankle had been feeling so much better recently that I had just spent a week presenting the Chelsea Flower Show, walking around for hours every day in flowery frocks and wedge heels. I was working. I had to. My feet had felt a little sore at the end of each day, but I put that down to the shoes. Nor will I mention that I danced all evening at the end of that week with the Chelsea Flower Show team. It was our last night in the showground, and Jo Whiley was on stage with her 90s anthems. It would have been rude not to. I had a few drinks. I couldn't feel my ankle at all. I may even have gone to the gym last week. A light deadlift or two. Right now though, I can tell by the tone of his voice that this is not information I should be volunteering. It's not going to change what he has seen on the scan. 'You must pull out of whatever you're doing immediately,' he says. 'Your bone is now fractured. You must take the weight off your ankle completely. That means a boot and crutches. Today.'

I am standing, croissant in hand, in the foyer of the hotel. A taxi is waiting outside to take me to the British Normandy memorial at Ver-sur-Mer for rehearsals ahead of tomorrow's long day of broadcasting at the Service of Remembrance. I am hot and I am cold. I can feel myself sweating. 'I can't pull out,' I tell him. 'I'm here for the D-Day anniversary. I've just crossed the Channel on a ferry with a group of 100-year-old veterans who've managed to make it here. I can't pull out because my ankle hurts a bit.' 'The scan shows your ankle is now broken. You are heading for an operation. You have to put yourself first right now, Sophie,' he says, sounding almost angry now. 'Do you understand me? Surely your employer can find you a boot and crutches today?' *Not out here, they can't*, I'm thinking. *Not right now in these Normandy villages with so much else going on ahead of tomorrow. Plus, it doesn't hurt at all really. So strange.* I don't quite believe him.

The taxi drops me at the entrance of the British memorial. It's a bit of a walk up to the white tents and trucks in the BBC compound and now I feel like I should be limping. I have a stress fracture, a broken ankle apparently. I burst into tears when I get to the production area and see people I know. My mind is a jumble. 'Is there anything you need?' asks Honey, one of the producers. 'Crutches,' I say. And she laughs, confused. Someone hands me a cup of tea, while I explain, flustered, what has just happened. I manage to pour the tea, made with hot water straight out of an urn, all over my hand, scalding my skin badly. That really does hurt. A first-aider appears by my side. 'Are you OK? What can I do?' 'Crutches. I need crutches,' I repeat again. Everyone looks baffled.

I'm shown into a dressing room in a marquee-like tent that's been set up for all the performers appearing tomorrow. Their names are pinned on black tarpaulin doors – Sir Tom Jones, Martin Freeman and Douglas Booth – and then there's me at the end. It's cold and I wrap myself in a blanket laid out on a chair. I've got lines to learn for something that I'm about to film, not many lines but the words won't stay in my head. I was so sure that my ankle was on the mend. How can it be broken? Honey, the producer, appears. She has found me some crutches. They belong to the Army. For some reason they have red ribbons dangling from them.

Crutches are exhausting. They really, really hurt your hands. I discover this about an hour later as I try to navigate a path through tightly parked TV trucks at Bayeux War Cemetery. This is where veterans and dignitaries are gathering on the eve of the D-Day anniversary for a Service of Remembrance. Princess Anne is there and I'm doing the first reading.

I've got to know a few of the veterans and their families after crossing the Channel with them on the ferry this week. These elderly men, frail, thin, some in wheelchairs, are all so determined to be here to remember their friends.

The youngest is 98. They wave and smile when they see me and then look completely confused when they spot the Army crutches. 'What have you done?' mouths one of them to me. It's too complicated to explain across the headstones of the Fallen. I feel ridiculous lurching around on crutches in front of these men who've survived unthinkable battle-day horrors. So, I ditch the crutches and walk up to the microphone slowly to do my reading. I'm not even limping, which must confuse them even more.

My next obstacles to overcome are a hedge, a ditch and a field. That is what I have to navigate, now back on crutches, to get to the makeshift podium on the edge of the cemetery from where I'll be presenting the *Six* and *Ten*. By now I am so cross that I've been ordered on to crutches that I refuse any help and push my way through the hedge, hop into the ditch, somehow scramble up it and nearly keel over on the other side before stumbling across lumpy grass, finally arriving red-faced with my team. There's a big director's chair by the platform, which Toby, one of the producers, has found somewhere and dragged here. 'Sit down,' he orders. 'You're not taking this seriously enough. You nearly went flying in that field. Don't you move!' He lets me stand up for the news though, which I deliver balancing on one foot.

The Army takes back the crutches as soon as the D-Day commemorations are over the next day. A man from the military tracks me down to my dressing room. He needs the crutches back, he says with a smile. He's sorry to take them off me, but I can't keep them. I leave the BBC compound at the British Normandy Memorial as I arrived – flummoxed and on two feet.

Back in London I am put in a fracture boot and on to new crutches. I feel broken, inside and out. Unable to sleep on my first day home, I hop downstairs in the middle of the night to get a drink and end up crawling back up on my hands and knees, crying. I should be flying down mountains. Now I can't even get up the stairs in my house.

A radiologist looks at the scans of my ankle. It is definitely broken. But he now says the stress fracture has been there all along. It was missed on the original scan and I have been walking around on a broken bone since the London Marathon. It is a rare injury. A stress fracture of the lateral process of the talus bone, a 'snowboarders' fracture', caused when the ankle is forced outwards. No one is very sure how I've managed to do it running. I cry again as one of the top ankle surgeons tells me it could take months to heal. 'We need to hit it hard,' he says. 'You must be non-weight-bearing for at least the next six to eight weeks and maybe beyond. And you may well need an operation at the end of this, however good you are at keeping your weight off it.'

I only realise many, many months later that it is almost certainly the carbon-plated shoes that I have trained so much in over the past 12 months that have left me with a fractured ankle. This is not something I will ever be able to prove for sure. I have trained hard over the past year, but I haven't dramatically increased my mileage. It has remained pretty much the same as before. And I have been following a training plan sent to me every month by my online coach, Jo Wilkinson. The only thing that has changed is my shoes. And they are very, very different to the traditional shoes that I'm used to.

Carbon-plated shoes were first introduced in 2016 by Nike, and all the other brands soon rushed to follow with their own versions. 'Supershoes', as they are called, were originally designed for elite marathon runners and they have helped propel so many to world-record times. They have a rigid carbon plate in the sole of the shoe which is combined with thick foam cushioning. 'Think of the foam as a trampoline and the carbon plate as a spring propelling you forwards. There's also a "rocker", embedded in the forefoot of the shoe, like a rolling pin or a rocking chair, that literally rolls you forward. That's pretty much what a supershoe is,' says the podiatrist Liam McManus, who will eventually try to get me back on my feet and help me recover from this injury. 'Supershoes throw you forward which is great for speed, but they put much more force through your mid and fore foot and that is a significant change for many runners. Bones, joints, tendons, muscles, ankles, knees – suddenly they're all being loaded differently. The question is can your body tolerate it?'

My body couldn't, as it turned out. I bought my first pair of carbon-plated shoes in 2019 and ran my fastest ever marathon. I loved them for their speed and bounce. They were expensive and didn't last long so I only wore them on race days. But in the autumn of 2023, when I set my sights on just one more PB, I trained in them a lot more – in races, at parkrun, in speed sessions during the week. And then a few months before the London Marathon, my ankle started to niggle. Carbon-plated shoes fundamentally change your gait and the way you run. The shoes also do a lot more of the work for you as you spring along, meaning your feet, ankles and lower limbs don't have to work quite as hard. But over time that weakens your muscles and tendons – your calves, your Achilles. That's not something that is talked about much. And the thick foamy soles in these high-stack shoes can also make your ankle far more unstable. There's very little support. No one had warned me of the injuries supershoes might cause if I overused them. 'Your foot doesn't move in supershoes,' Liam McManus explains to me. 'If you train in them more than you should do, you are weakening your intrinsic muscles. Making sure that your feet and lower limbs are strong enough to withstand the force is crucial.' I hadn't been aware of any of that. And now I am panicking. My pursuit of speed and a few minutes off my PB may mean I can never run again. Right now, I can't even walk without help.

The practicalities of life on crutches confound me. How do you make a cup of tea and get it across the kitchen from the kettle to the table when you're hopping on one leg? It is impossible to do without putting my injured foot on the ground. Non-weight-bearing becomes my new challenge. I take it on like marathon training. I order new kit: a backpack with lots of pockets and insulated mugs that I can carry tea and coffee around in without any spillage. I call Fiona Bruce, my friend and BBC colleague, who broke her ankle a few years ago in a freak accident at a trampoline park with her daughter. An operation meant she couldn't put her injured foot down on the ground at all for at least four months. She had sped around the newsroom on some wheeled contraption, much to our amusement. 'You have to get a knee scooter,' she cries. 'It's got a padded seat for you to kneel on. You need to get a basket on the front to carry things. It'll transform your life. I went dog walking on mine. And you must get gel pads for your crutches to save your hands. I'm sending you a YouTube video right now to show you how to get upstairs more easily on crutches.'

Work is a challenge too. The 2024 general election is just a month away and I am hosting the Leaders' Debate between Rishi Sunak and Sir Keir Starmer in three weeks' time. The format is standing up with the two party leaders facing me at a podium. The debate is at least an hour and a half long. I'm getting good at balancing on one foot but I'm not sure I can do it for a full 90 minutes under pressure. The issue is not just physical. Being injured has dented my confidence much more than I thought it would. I am surprised by just how deeply it affects me. I need to be on top of my game to do this debate and right now I feel far from that. I feel broken. I talk to my boss and tell him that I can't do it. Not like this. I pull out. My colleague, Mishal Husain, will do it instead. 'Come back to work though,' says John, my editor on the *Six* and *Ten*. 'You can still do the news. It will be fine. We will work around you. Just come back. We want you here.'

My daily challenge becomes getting around. I refuse to take a taxi to work and insist on still taking the tube. A neighbour lends me a knee scooter. The first time I take it out I am too ambitious. I put my backpack on, take the dog, buy a coffee on the way to the park. Then one of the thin plastic front wheels catches a kerb and I go flying in the middle of a busy junction, landing hard on my knee and gashing my hand. Motorists stare. A cyclist looks aghast and rushes to pick me up. I am more embarrassed than hurt. I decide to buy my own scooter, one with bigger, chunky 'off-road' front wheels. At least that way I have a chance of staying upright. A quick search online takes me straight to Victoria Beckham on a bright green one. It was a present from David, it says on her Instagram page, when she broke her foot in the gym. She's wearing a baseball cap, all dressed in black, and she has a cupholder on the handlebars. She manages to make knee scooters look cool. It's going to cost me more than £200 but if that means I can get the tube rather than a taxi, it'll be saving me a lot of money in the end.

There's no lift or escalator at my local tube station. Just a wooden staircase. I stop at the bottom of the three flights, look up and take a deep breath. I've climbed these steps so many times before. I haven't yet worked out my strategy for getting to the top now, on one foot with a scooter in tow. I'm relying once again on the kindness of strangers, and within minutes someone steps forward and asks if they can help. They grab the scooter. I hop up behind them, counting as I go. One hundred steps to the top. The muscles in my right leg are burning.

I get quite speedy as the weeks pass by, much to the amusement of my colleagues at work who look up and laugh as I whizz and weave through the desks in the newsroom. I present the news sitting down all the time: no roaming between the big screens in the studio. No one seems to notice that I'm not moving.

Dog walks on my new all-terrain scooter become much speedier. We now have a new dog, Luna. She is exactly the same kind of dog as Winnie, but a different colour, fox red, not black, and a bit bigger. We found her soon after Winnie died. Replacing her felt like a betrayal but slowly Luna helped patch up the pain. And like Winnie, it turned out that she loved to run, though not after squirrels or car wheels or bicycles, thankfully. Now, I put Luna into her Canicross kit, a special harness and elasticated lead on a belt designed for dog and runner. Except I attach her to the handlebars of my knee scooter instead of my waist. She gets the idea quickly and learns to pull me to the park. 'Mush, mush,' I shout as we go, laughing. There are small triumphs every day. I go to the gym for upper body-only exercises on a quest to be able to do more than one pull-up. However, it's not long before I see myself in the *Daily Mail* having been 'papped' by a photographer who must have been tipped off that they'd get an amusing photo of me on a green scooter if they waited outside long enough. That one picture puts me off struggling through any more one-footed, arm-busting exercises for a while. I finally give myself up to the non-weight-bearing life and wait it out.

---

Four months after the London Marathon I am finally allowed to put my foot on the ground again. I am at least half a stone heavier. My recovery starts very slowly, with my toes. My physio, Sue Donnelly, tells me to sit on the floor and orders me to lift up my little toe on my bad foot all on its own. I can't. It lies there like a tiny paralysed limb. It's weird to see. I stare at it, willing it to move. Nothing happens. We try my big toe next. I have never studied my toes this much. The more I look at my big toe, the more I think of a tortoise's head poking out of its shell. Sue, blue-eyed, smiley, charming and Irish, tells me to keep my big toe firmly on the floor and lift all the others up one after the other, a kind of toe wave. Not bad on my good foot, almost impossible on my recently broken one. And my little toe still won't move.

'Why am I having to do this?' I moan. 'What's this to do with running?!' 'It's all about improving your basic foot control and strength,' she says, smiling encouragingly, not allowing me to stop. 'Being able to control your foot better after your fracture will help you manage the load as you start running again. We want to make sure this doesn't happen again.' She sends me off with my homework. Toe control practice. Calf raises too. Lots of them every day.

My first run back is extreme and short. I am back in the Alps again at the end of August for the UTMB week in Chamonix, this time with Susie. We were supposed to be running the OCC together, her first mountain race. But Susie's terror of heights means she has refused to do it without me. She has never been to the Alps before and is too worried about finding herself paralysed by vertigo on some alpine slope. Instead, we have decided to come here, spectate and do a bit of running, so she can at least get a feel for it and see if she wants to run one of the races next year. We head out on the first morning along a gentle path following a river to test out my ankle. I manage 5km without stopping for the first time since April. My foot feels better the further I go. My lungs, on the other hand, are raging. My heart rate is sky-high. 'This is so hard!' I gasp to Susie, who is skipping along easily beside me. 'We are at altitude, Soph,' she laughs. 'You're not exactly making this return to running easy for yourself. Don't worry. You'll get your fitness back soon.'

Chamonix in race week is glorious. Big screens all over the town show live coverage of the elite runners thousands of feet above us in the snow-capped mountains. Trail runners and mountain bikers carry cameras and livestream every step of the big three races – 50km, 100km and the main 170km race. It must be the only ultra race that you can experience fully, while watching from a seat in the sunshine with a coffee in hand. There's a commentary team that works around the clock for five days following the leaders in each race. The main UTMB race sets off at 6 p.m. on Friday at the end of the week and we are whisked into the mountains to try to track the elites after they set off from Chamonix, heading in a circle all the way around Mont Blanc. The lead runners will take around 20 hours to complete the whole thing. The last finishers will take two days to get back to base. The villages all along the route are packed and there's a carnival atmosphere, restaurants and bars heaving with people cheering on the 2000 runners who keep streaming past for hours.

The elites come piling through. We marvel at their pace and then we speed off ahead again by car to try to catch them before darkness descends. At Notre-Dame de la Gorge, 35km into the race, the path narrows on the first steep climb into the mountains. The noise is insane as we approach. Music, flares, huge flags, thousands of people on a path so narrow I think it must be a parallel route. But the roars behind me make me turn, and suddenly there they are, the lead runners pushing up hard and fast behind me. We can touch them, they are that close. A tunnel of arms and bodies and cheers all around them as they push through us all and up off into the stillness of night in the mountains.

I feel wistful, a little sad. I wish my body could carry me along those mountain trails right now. Instead, I have a long path of rehab ahead that will need huge amounts of patience.

The next morning, I run again with Susie along the river path and then push on a little further as I head back into town. It is wonderful to be out with my friend again. My exhilaration is dented though when I am overtaken by runners who've been racing all night, on their way to the finish line. They are exhausted after more than 100km in the mountains, but they are still moving better than I am. Fitness fades frighteningly fast, I realise. I am back on that track. One foot in front of the other. But will I ever be able to run like I used to again?

## 13
## *The circle of life*

It is New Year's Day. I am sitting in the downstairs loo at a friend's house in Berkshire. The morning after the night before and my head hurts. I'm dehydrated. I don't know why I'm not still asleep. On the wall is a picture, a drawing of a river that I start to study more carefully. The Thames, 'From the Source to the Sea', it says in smaller letters underneath. The sketch by William Thomas twists and turns in great swirls through places I know well: Oxford, Windsor, Richmond and on into London. This mighty river has flowed through my entire life. I grew up within feet of it in Richmond; my parents still live close to its banks, as do I, further downstream in London.

I see the Thames most days. I have run its riverbanks so often that I can reel off the distances between many of its bridges. But what I hadn't fully understood until now, as I stare at the drawing on the wall, is that the Thames begins more than 180 miles from London, near Cirencester in Gloucestershire. The drawing doesn't say exactly where but it won't be hard to find. It is 1 January 2019, and I decide, in my hungover state, that my New Year's resolution will be to run from the source of the Thames all the way to the sea. It's 232 miles in total. It will have to be done in stages, not all in one go. But I know who will want to come with me: Susie, Shaun and the gang.

A few months later, in May 2019, we pile out of a train at Kemble station in Gloucestershire and jog slowly in the direction of the field on my map that's marked 'Source of the River Thames (spring)'. It's almost 2 miles from the station. We go slowly. We have a long run ahead. We climb over a stile and arrive in the middle of the field. There's a big rock, waist-height, on a plinth. A stone to mark the source of the river. Next to it is a wooden signpost pointing south. 'Thames Path' it says, and underneath, 'Thames Barrier London 184 miles'. As for the river itself, there is not a single drop of water in sight. Nothing. The ground isn't even wet. How can this be the start of such a powerful force that pours its way through so much of southern England and out into the North Sea? I keep looking for water. I still can't quite believe there isn't any. 'This is a bit like how you and I started running all those years ago,' I joke to Susie, as we scour the ground. 'Very underwhelming at the start, very unexpected. No inkling at all of what was to come and where it would take us!' She rolls her eyes at me and laughs. 'Yes! And look what we turned into!'

Six of us set off across the field following the waterless Thames Path. We have to run almost half a mile before we find anything watery at all. There's a cow and a big, messy, swampy puddle at the far end of the next field, more grass and then the smallest of trickles curving around a bend. We all stop in the meadow and stare at the beginnings of the infant river.

The Thames starts in humble ways. Soon it is a small stream, glassy, so clear that we can see the riverbed. It runs

## THE CIRCLE OF LIFE

through fields, past woodland into small Cotswold villages, remarkable mainly because of the force we know this water will hold, not now but dozens of miles downstream. For the first 20 miles or so the infant river is not navigable. It's not deep enough for most boats. It feels remote, wild out here on meadow paths. We see very few people but plenty of horses, sheep and cows.

I like exploring like this, discovering new places, running from point to point on a mission rather than training over the same, often repetitive routes. We have no time pressure here. I dip in and out of the chat around me as the miles rack up and watch the water, in search of hints of its might and energy ahead.

Our first Thames section ends in Lechlade on the edge of the Cotswolds, where the river has turned from a puddle into a stream into a steady flow that is now 60 feet wide. We find a pub by the water and collapse after a long 24 miles, wolfing down chips and poring over the map to plot the next stage of our Thames Path run. Getting home is harder. We have to find a seven-seater cab to take us all on the 10-mile journey to Swindon, the nearest station, and a train home.

Ticking off the Thames Path turns into a slow process. But then this is not a project I need to hurry. Susie and I go back a month later in June and then again in July. Lechlade to Newbridge, then Newbridge to Oxford, are the next sections, adding up to another 30 miles. Much of it we run alone, through remote fields, this time dotted with red poppies that stand strikingly in among green crops. The river is no longer young. It is swelling and flowing with purpose now as it heads towards its first city, Oxford. Susie and I push each other on along the paths, as we did in the Sahara, following each other's heels, on a journey that started the day we met thousands of miles over the Atlantic on our way to the Boston Marathon.

Beyond Oxford come Abingdon and Wallingford and then the river flanks the Chiltern Hills as it passes through Goring, Pangbourne and on to the pretty market town of Henley. We run through them all, drawn inexorably onwards as the river wends its way towards London and beyond.

---

The Chilterns are where I find myself years later, in 2025, as I return to running following my ankle injury, unsure if I have lost my ability to play the long game, to run far. And as ever, Susie is to blame for me being there.

The most ridiculous thing you can do when you are just back from injury is run an ultramarathon without doing any other races in between. 'I'm doing the Centurion Hundred Hills race in March if anyone fancies it? 50k?' Susie types in our runners' WhatsApp group at the start of 2025. I say nothing but I google it. It involves 31 miles and 4500 feet of climbing across the Chilterns, two 15-mile loops up and over 17 hills. It's not one hundred hills as billed, which comes as a bit of a relief. 'Hundred Hills' turns out to be the name of a small vineyard near the start line in Stonor Park in Oxfordshire. The race is three months off and I've just started marathon training again. My ankle is holding up, just about. I have good weeks and not-so-good weeks. But I can run again now. I sign up to the ultra without telling Susie. *Keep it quiet*, I think to myself. I can always pull out.

March comes around fast. Marathon training has been OK. I'm up to 18 miles now, though my legs can only just cope with hills. I am running much slower than a year ago. I don't push it. There is a lingering fear. I finally tell my coach, Jo, what I've signed up for, expecting her to be horrified and insist I don't do it. 'Well, OK,' she says calmly after a pause. 'So, walk up the hills, enjoy it, get your confidence back. And if your ankle is hurting, just stop at the end of the first loop.' This was not the reaction I had been expecting. Now I actually have to do this race. I tell Susie that I am coming with her. She screeches in excitement down the phone. 'But, but, but,' I plough on, 'under no circumstances can you wait for me. I will be slow. I don't want the pressure. I may only make it half-way round.'

Injury plays on your mind, pokes at your confidence even once you know you are fixed. Before my fracture, I was sure my body was strong. In my mind, sore muscles and aching tendons were part of the strengthening process. Now each twinge makes me fearful that I may break once more. I worry often that I won't ever feel strong again. Unexpectedly it is a ballet dancer who resets my mind and gives me some of my confidence back.

Steven McRae is a principal at the Royal Ballet. In 2019, on stage at the Royal Opera House, he took off for a jump and his Achilles snapped mid-air. He heard it go. *Was there a piece of wood on the floor beneath him?* he wondered fleetingly as he heard the loud noise. Then he landed and the pain hit. Two-and-a-half thousand people were watching as he fell to the floor and screamed. He tried to get up, he tried to keep dancing, but realised he literally did not have a leg to stand on. The curtain came down on the show. On his career too. At least that was what he was thinking as he was carried off to his dressing room.

I first met Steven five years later at a private screening of a new BBC documentary, *Dancing Back to the Light*, that had followed his recovery. He had had surgery to repair his Achilles and was left in a cast. 'I kind of feel useless,' he says in the film after he has climbed the stairs on crutches. It took a full year before he felt even semi-confident to walk again. A whole year. I recognised that feeling of uselessness, of having your physical strength just taken away. Without it my confidence had been knocked, quite profoundly. But dancing was Steven McRae's life and he was not going to give up. His determination and bloody-mindedness that shone through in the documentary was incredible to watch, and deeply moving. Two years of recovery and intense rehab and he was dancing again. A changed man, a changed body that will need strengthening forever. But he made it back to doing what he loves, what empowers him.

Two days before the Hundred Hills ultramarathon, I was invited to watch Steven in rehearsals for the Royal Ballet's *Romeo and Juliet*, a three-hour ballet that he was performing that Saturday at Covent Garden. It was the same day that I was going to run. In the years since his Achilles ruptured, he had also snapped a major tendon in the other knee, his anterior cruciate ligament or ACL. And yet he leapt and spun and moved around the rehearsal studio lifting the Ukrainian ballerina, Iana Salenko, with ease. I winced every time he landed and marvelled at the courage it took for him to put his body under so much pressure after two such major injuries. 'Steven, don't look at the top of the mountain or you will slip on the pebbles,' said his coach, Leanne Benjamin, during rehearsals. I smiled as she said it and made a mental note to remember that at the weekend.

I wished Steven luck as I left the rehearsals, explaining that I couldn't be at the performance itself on Saturday afternoon as I was running the Hundred Hills ultra. I told him how worried I had been about doing it but that watching him had filled me with a new determination to get out there and give it a go. 'Let's just hope we both make it through and out the other side on Saturday afternoon,' he said, laughing. 'Anything is possible. That's what I always say. Anything is possible. Just give it a go; you'll see.'

On the day of the race, I am surprisingly, unusually calm. It is the most beautiful cloudless blue-sky spring day. I drive into Stonor Park early, following the line of cars carrying runners to the start. I have my backpack stuffed with energy gels and snacks to help get me through the day. I've brought my running poles too for extra support to power me up the hills. It is a relief to feel no pressure at all. I've told no one except my running gang that I'm here and I have no pace to stick to. I'm enjoying being back on a race start line, soaking up all the nervous energy.

About 500 of us set off from beneath the inflatable arch on what is the warmest day of the year so far. The trails are perfect and dry. No mud in sight. We start climbing quickly on a path I realise I have run before. It's a long, slow grind to the top past a farm and through woodland filled with beech. I manage to stay close to Susie and Shaun as they bound along up ahead with a friend they've bumped into. They all look so much fitter and stronger than I feel. Shaun 'the Rock' drops back to check on me. He doesn't say that's what he's doing, but I know him well. 'Do not wait for me, honestly,' I tell him. 'I'll be fine. I'm going at my own pace today.' I keep them in sight for 14 miles and then just as we are heading back into Stonor Park for the next checkpoint and the start of the second 15-mile loop, I watch as they sail off up a hill. Without looking back, they disappear into the distance.

I love the second loop. I see my car parked up near the checkpoint and I am not tempted for a moment to stop. The trails are spectacular through woods, across fields, in and out of chocolate-box villages. I tick off the hills as we climb them. The aid stations are manned by smiling volunteers helping fill our drinks bottles and offering up lots of food. As we climb out of the village of Hambleden, just a mile from the Thames, I find myself running alongside a man called Ray from Ireland, who tells me he hasn't been feeling well but decided to give it a go anyway. He was expecting to do this course in under five hours but flu got the better of him. Now he just wants to finish. *Five hours?* I think to myself. *That's fast. He's a good runner. And I'm right here with him.* It gives me a little boost, a little fire.

I look at my watch. We are about to hit 20 miles. 'This is the furthest I've run in a year,' I tell him, beaming, and we both cheer. Twenty miles. The last time I ran this far I limped off the London Marathon course. Now I'm flying down the Chiltern Hills. I smile a lot during that second loop. *I will walk to the end if I have to,* I keep thinking, though my legs are feeling stronger than expected after all the gym work I've been doing. I fall into step with a man from Ealing. I never discover his name. But we play cat and mouse as we march up and run down the hills. He's stronger on the ups. I'm stronger on the downs. 'See you shortly,' he laughs every time he overtakes me on the climbs. The hardest parts of the race are the few flat stretches on tarmac, when I just have to grind it out.

As I climb up a wooded path towards the last checkpoint at 28 miles, I suddenly recognise the fields and a fallen tree that Fiona Bruce had jumped over on her horse just a couple of months ago. I was with her, out on horseback for the first time in years, and declined to take that leap, in case it ended in tears. I decided to cheer her on instead. Now, here I am, back on familiar ground with Bix Common opening up ahead. Volunteers by the small village hall, the last checkpoint, start cheering me on. 'If you want to stop, it's this way,' shouts a woman when I get close. 'Stop?' I say, aghast. 'I'm not stopping now! I'm almost there!' 'No, I meant stop for some food or water,' she replies, laughing. They pour Coca-Cola into my plastic drinks bottle. A rush of sugar and I'm off on the final few miles.

*Anything is possible.* That is what I start repeating over and over again in my head. *Anything is possible. Don't stop, don't slow down, keep running, no walking.* Thirty miles beeps on my watch. *Keep running. Anything is possible.* It's 3 p.m. I've been out here for more than six hours now. I think of Steven McRae on stage at Covent Garden and hope he's still going too. One last climb and then the finish line appears in the distance. I'm on my own now. No other runners near me. I have no idea how far down the pack I am. I just need to get there now. I can see the cars lined up in Stonor Park and hear the loudspeaker at the inflatable arch. I run and run and run until I'm off the trails and back on to the road where a volunteer is standing, pointing me to the end. 'There's not a cruel lap of Stonor Park to do before the finish is there? That really is the finish, just there?' I ask, gasping for breath. He laughs. 'You're there! You've done it!'

Dozens of people start shouting my name as I run the final few metres of the race. Six hours and 15 minutes, it says on the clock. A long day out on my feet. Susie is there waiting, with a medal around her neck. She and Shaun had got back 10 minutes before me. I run straight into her arms, swallowing down a great sob. 'I spent a lot of last year thinking I'd never run like this again,' I mumble and then burst into tears.

Susie and I have finished 24th and 25th out of more than 100 women. I am third in my 55-plus age group, a reminder of that lesson I learnt in the desert seven years ago: that the body is so much stronger than the mind lets you believe. There's a tent with tea and food and chairs. I can't sit down. I can't bend down. I can't stop smiling. My legs keep cramping but post-race euphoria is kicking in. I've missed the race-day endorphins. I'd forgotten just how good they make me feel. I send a photo of me clutching my colourful Hundred Hills medal to Steven McRae. 'Thank you for inspiring me. I spent a lot of the race saying "anything is possible" over and over again. A year ago, I didn't know if I'd run again.' He replies with photos of him leaping through the air on stage.

## THE CIRCLE OF LIFE

'Congratulations, Sophie! Truly incredible! I survived the performance too!'

The drive home from the race takes me across the Thames again at Henley, over the bridge by the rowing clubs and the famous Henley Royal Regatta course. I sit in a queue of traffic waiting to cross the bridge and look out at this section of the river that I remember ticking off on my Thames Path mission more than five years ago now.

---

This stretch around Henley is known as Middle Thames and it winds from here more than 20 miles to Windsor Castle. It's wide now and in full flow, impressive in scale but still calm, passing Georgian buildings and vast river-front mansions.

I ran along this section of the Thames Path on New Year's Eve 2019, 17 miles from Henley to Maidenhead along the muddy banks, through Cookham, past Marlow with its picturesque suspension bridge and on to the bend in the river overlooked by the impressive Italianate mansion, Cliveden House, once home to the Astors, now a country hotel. Its grounds slope down to the water where motor-boats cruise by.

During the last days of 2019 and the first few of the New Year I am consumed by ticking off new sections of the path on my journey to the sea. These are my fastest running days, as it turns out. At the age of 51 I am bagging marathon and half marathon PBs, running well, feeling strong. The Thames journey adds endurance to my fitness. I don't know why but I feel an urgency to get it done, to make it to London and the Thames Barrier. It will pay off because once I get there, Covid will be about to shut the world down.

The palaces by the Thames start at Hampton Court. This is home territory now. I grew up around here and know this stretch of the river inside out, but I run it again anyway. Teddington is where the Thames finally becomes tidal after its more than 150-mile journey from Gloucestershire. Beyond Teddington Lock, a car park by the 17th-century Ham House, overlooked by Richmond Park, is the finish line for a marathon of a different kind that I've completed twice now.

The Great River Race is a river marathon raced by hundreds of crews from Millwall in East London beyond Tower Bridge back here to Ham, under 28 bridges in the opposite direction to my river run. Boats of all shapes and sizes, crews of all levels, many racing, many others in fancy dress out there for fun and to raise money for charity. I rowed it with my father as part of an eight-strong crew in a skerry, a cross between two traditional Thames boats: a skiff and a wherry. Dad, ever one for a challenge, was in his 70s when I first stepped on board. He had already done the race before. Now, he was newly diagnosed with Parkinson's disease that within years would waste his legs away so much that his limbs would look like the boat's thin wooden oars. I went along the third time he insisted on doing it, mainly to reassure my mother that he would get out of the boat alive. He did, though as we passed under Richmond Bridge with just a short distance to go before the finish at Ham House, Parkinson's caused Dad to freeze and he couldn't row any more. We had to pretty much carry him out of the boat at the end.

## THE CIRCLE OF LIFE

Now, at the start of 2025, both my parents are in their early 80s and neither is able to walk very far. Dad, despite his determination and stubbornness of an ox, has been hollowed out by disease. It has taken away his strength, a lot of his mind and now much of his voice. This giant of a man who raced me down black slopes on skis in the Alps and spent years on the London Marathon finish line cheering me on with tears in his eyes, now struggles to stand. I take my parents' rapid physical decline personally, acutely aware of how quickly it has come on. Two years is all it has taken for them to go from slow and a bit wobbly to almost no movement at all. I am also not getting any younger. Now in my late 50s, this constantly plays on my mind.

*How will I age?* I wonder, as I watch my shrunken parents in wheelchairs. *They didn't exercise like I do. They weren't running marathons in their 50s. Will exercise protect me from what they are going through or am I destined for the same trajectory?*

From Richmond Lock bridge, the Thames path begins a curvy rise and fall, like a double-humped camel, past Kew Gardens, Chiswick Bridge, flowing through Barnes and under Hammersmith's famous suspension bridge. This is my training ground. These are the flat riverbanks where I first set off, lungs burning, with my husband and two tiny children in a double buggy two decades ago. Humble beginnings, like this river. I never imagined where those first runs would lead me. Those children are now adults, good runners too, though they tell me I put them off years ago by repeatedly dragging them to parkrun. Now they are starting to discover on their own the satisfaction of getting out there, the power of a run.

My running companion along these stretches of the river is mostly Luna. She comes back when I call her, she stays close to my heels. Her obsession is balls, or a stick will do. She's not interested in squirrels. I take her out often on 5-mile runs around the Thames bridges. We have a routine. She finds a stick, carries it, glances longingly at me until I give in and stop to throw it. Five throws is the deal, then we run on again, both of us happy. She can go a long way on small legs. Ten miles is the furthest I take her, though she always seems to have the energy to go on.

Putney Bridge is where the rush of London begins, the river traffic, the large Thames Clippers that ferry commuters and tourists from here into the heart of the city, carried on the flow to Westminster and the Houses of Parliament, Waterloo, Tower Bridge, Canary Wharf and beyond to the Thames Barrier. This is where the noise, power and intensity of the river are in full force, where the water turns brackish, salt from the North Sea finally infiltrating the freshwater flow. And this is where the final few miles of the London Marathon are played out every year in front of screaming crowds, a cacophony of noise and excitement, along the river's Embankment.

---

A year after I limped off the course at mile 20, I am back and ready to run, though I am a lot slower than last year. The 2025 London Marathon will be my 12th. This time it has been all about getting to the start line uninjured and completing it. I have done the training, enough to get round in under 4 hours, hopefully. I am nervous about the distance, about the pressure I put myself under every year to get a good time. I'm a little anxious too about my ankle, though it has been pain-free since I completely stopped running in carbon-plated shoes some months ago. With two days to go, I collect my race number from the Expo centre in the Docklands, weaving through the vast crowds. Around 56,000 people are running it this year.

And then suddenly I find myself in a marathon of a very different kind.

That night, the Friday before the London Marathon, my 83-year-old father Richard enters the final stretches of his life. This man, adored by so many, has finally been stripped of the ability to swallow by the disease that has been slowly invading his body for more than a decade now. He is in bed, unable to walk or speak or eat or drink. In the last week Parkinson's has even robbed Dad of the ability to smile. He always smiled, my dad. A big, welcoming, warm, embracing smile. I find the fact that he can't now smile devastating, though there is something in his eyes that still dances a little when he's trying. His only way to communicate is by blinking or lifting his hand. At times he only has the strength to move his thumb. My sister, Kate, makes him two paper signs – 'YES' and 'NO' in big black letters. 'Do you want to go to hospital, Dad?' we ask him yet again, this time in front of a GP who has come to assess him. He raises one hand and swipes hard at 'NO'. He has been adamant for a long time now that he wants to stay at home. I have been on too many trips to A&E in the back of ambulances with him recently, blue lights flashing. The latest was just last week.

On Saturday morning when I should be laying out my marathon-running kit and counting out my energy gels for the race, I throw a few clothes into a bag and head back to my childhood home by the Thames instead. My sister and I settle in around a hospital bed that's been set up in our parents' room. We throw open the windows and let the sunlight stream in. From where he lies, he can see the trees in the rose-filled garden that he and our mother created from nothing more than 50 years ago. Our mother, also unable to walk and with medical problems of her own, is struggling to process what is going on and spends most of the time downstairs. Throughout my whole life, I have always known that my father would drop everything for me instantly. Now I do the same for him.

I watch the London Marathon on television for the first time since 2010 when I'd seen Jenni Falconer cross the finish line and thought, *I am going to do that next year.* Dad had been there on The Mall ready to cheer me on with Mum, Richard and the kids. And then, of course, I had collapsed and for hours he was worried sick not knowing what had happened to me. Now, 14 years later, he is the one in a hospital bed at home. And I am the one desperately worrying about his racing heart rate as he fights for breath. At least I know where he is.

For six whole days he lives on without any food or water. We don't leave his side, keeping vigil day and night. He knows we are there. He hears our voices. His eyes open sometimes, not for long. He stares straight ahead. We don't know if he can see us, but we rush to him just in case, leaning right over him to reassure him. Family and neighbours come and go, cups of tea around his bed. Glasses of wine in his room to the sounds of jazz that he played with my sister in their neighbourhood band many years ago now. Kate sings. We drink. We dance to the soundtrack of our childhood. Every Sunday evening, jazz in someone's house. A band that began decades ago, a community coming together to help my father deal with his terrible depression, when he was first diagnosed with bipolar disorder in the 1980s. Music to lift his spirits. A community holding each other up. But now John, the pianist, is gone, Michael, the double bass player, and Robin, the saxophonist, too. Peter, who played the drums, died a long time ago now. Dad, the bass guitar player, and Kate, the singer, are the last two survivors. Now he is about to go as well. We watch Dad for signs that he can hear us singing and imagine that he is probably concentrating hard on playing the bass line in his head. 'Isn't it strange,' says Kate, 'that we will never be able to ask him if he knows we are here, if he knows that we didn't leave him.'

My parents bought this house when I was six years old. There is a whole community that wants to say goodbye. I marvel at the strength of Dad's emaciated body. The stubborn determination of his mind. The fight to live against all the odds. Powering on in his last miles. Such resilience, digging deep, holding on until his own finish line. His hands are warm to the very end. He had a huge heart, this man. Great humour. Deep kindness. This is what everyone keeps telling us. 'Ah Sophie – I love your father. Such a warrior and tenacious lover of life,' texts Franny Alagiah, George's widow, when I warn her that my dad is on his way out. 'Talk to him in his ear, Sophie. Please send him my love and ask him to greet George.' I whisper her words. He blinks a lot behind closed eyes.

A fox wanders through the garden in broad daylight. Its head is reddish, its back and tail silvery. It pees in the middle of my father's prized lawn. Dad would have been furious and chased it off by now. I watch as it heads to the corner of the garden and balances carefully on rocks so that it can dip its narrow muzzle into the cool water of the pond and drink. It drinks and drinks and drinks. It is such a long drink. I glance back at Dad, asleep in a haze of morphine behind me. He hasn't been able to swallow a drop of water for six days and nights now. Then the silver fox turns and saunters back across the wooden bridge over Dad's bog garden, pees on that too, spraying the purple primulas, before heading casually across the lawn again and past the back door under a huge archway of yew that my parents planted half a century ago.

That night my father dies. It is 1.35 a.m. on 1 May 2025 when he takes his last breath. My sister, who has been sleeping next to him all night, wakes me. 'He's gone, Soph,' she says. After years of having his body disturbed and disrupted by Parkinson's disease, he is finally still. He looks so different in death, I think. Handsome, thinner, younger, such a thick head of hair, like Marlon Brando. It has been a most peaceful death.

My sister and I go outside in the pitch black and sit on the brick path, overlooking the lawn, under a canopy of stars. It's 4 a.m. The only light is from our parents' room one floor up. The curtains are open. We make a small fire in a tin plant container and burn sticks that Kate has gathered from the garden for this moment, to send him on his way. The wood crackles, the flames leap. Dad's water sprinklers burst into life in the flower bed next to us. The sudden sound of water makes us jump and then laugh. 'We're not burning your garden down, Dad, don't worry,' I say with a smile, looking up at the light in the room where he now lies dead. In the darkness a tawny owl suddenly calls out twice with a quavering *hoo hu-hooo, hoo hu-hoooo*. A lone male letting it be known to the females nearby that he is here. 'That's Dad,' I say to Kate. A silver fox and a wise owl.

Our father leaves our family home for the last time that afternoon, carried out by two undertakers on a stretcher wrapped in maroon sheets. I've given them a rose from his garden to tuck in there. We gather at the gate to see him go. Mum, looking stunned, is wheeled out by her carers. She has hardly spoken since he died. I haven't seen her cry. They would have been married for 59 years in the summer. My husband brings a bottle of champagne and glasses. Two neighbours from across the road come and join us. Irene, who has lived in this street even longer than us, is also in her mid-80s, fragile and crying. Her husband Michael, the band's double bass player, had died suddenly less than a year ago. I worry that she's about to collapse. We fetch her a chair from the kitchen and bring it out on to the pavement.

Dad goes out of the front door for the last time, carried under the wisteria in full bloom that he has spent decades training up the front of the house. Down the path lined with pyramids of box hedge that he has nurtured and shaped for years. To the gate where we are all standing, champagne glasses in hand. We raise our glasses as he is loaded into a private ambulance. Dad, always the most generous host. 'I never managed to come to your house without your dad offering me a glass of wine,' says Irene through tears. Kate and I stand in the middle of the street. Dad always insisted on coming to wave us off from the pavement every time we drove away. 'Keep waving to Grandpa, kids,' I would always say until he disappeared completely from view. Even last week he had made it to the gate one last time with a Zimmer frame and a wheelchair being pushed behind him, just in case. As the ambulance pulls away, Kate and I stand in the middle of the road and wave and wave and wave until it disappears from view.

And then he is gone.

I run. I run because I can. I run because it makes me feel alive. I run to stay strong, to live long. I run to the water, to the banks of the flowing Thames, under Richmond Bridge and on into Richmond Park through Petersham Gate where I climb the steep hill towards Pembroke Lodge in honour of my dad who obsessively power walked up this slope every week, until Parkinson's stopped him walking at all. *Don't stop*, I keep thinking. *Run right to the very top. For him.* Then it's back into Richmond past the famous view from the top of Richmond Hill and down into Queensberry Place, a stone's throw from the Thames, where I spent the first five years of my life in a small and pretty terraced house. A whole life by this river.

'When I die,' says my mother, who is struggling to process what is happening, 'I want to be scattered with Dad in the Thames and float out into the sea.'

---

It is 47.5 miles from the Thames Barrier to the sea along a new stretch of path that wasn't open when Susie and I first started out on our river run six years ago. The King

Charles III England Coast Path will eventually extend 2700 miles along the entire coast of England. It will be the longest managed coastal path in the world. When we had set out from Gloucestershire in 2019, there was still no public access to some sections on the last stretch to the coast. We would have had to divert inland. Now though, in 2025, Natural England, the public body that protects and restores England's landscapes, has negotiated with landowners. Almost all of our route will be by the water. Only some land owned by the Ministry of Defence is still off limits.

We leave London behind and run on into new lands unexplored by us all. Oystercatchers cry above dying industrial cityscapes. Wasted human rubbish lies in piles along the Thames Path. Between Woolwich and Erith on the border of Kent hangs the stench of sewage from one of Europe's biggest treatment plants. Discarded human effluent from more than 1.5 million people is treated and pumped into the river right here. A solitary birdwatcher is positioned, binoculars in hand, by a huge discharge pipe. It is strangely full of life. Birds dive down into the water. I stop, transfixed, and watch. 'The sewage plant draws in the fish. It's cleanish here,' says the man as we both stare down at the liquid gushing out into the river.

These are the frayed edges of the city, the land of metal recycling plants that line this stretch of the Thames. Wrecked cars piled high, empty shells crushed. Some older models have clearly reached the end of their life; others have been taken out far too soon. Dents in doorways, crumpled rooftops, smashed-in bonnets. Dead cars. I wonder whether their owners are still here with stories to tell. This is not the river's pretty face. Wading birds pick their way across mudflats in front of the scrap metal sites. Humanity has scarred this stretch of the Thames with its disregard for nature. Green mounds that rise up on the opposite shore are not natural. They are landfill sites, covered over with grass to hide discarded buried rubbish.

The river has more than doubled in size since we left London. In the distance the vast QE2 bridge spans the water carrying tens of thousands of vehicles across the river every day. It has to be high to allow all the ocean-going ships to pass underneath it. The water here is now salt water that has pushed up into the estuary, mixing with the fresh water flowing out the other way. This is where the river finally leaves London behind. Kent's boundary, ever shifting like the tide, has been nudged further and further out towards the sea over the years by the sprawling capital. By the time we reach Dartford we are firmly in the 'Garden of England', Kent County with its lush green landscape and orchards, though there is no sign of that here.

I start the final stretch of my Thames Path run from Gravesend, fitting, just weeks after Dad's funeral. This is where the marshlands begin. I have come a long way since the rock in the dry field at the river's source in Gloucestershire. For this last leg of the journey, I am on my own. Susie wanted to come with me to finish off what we both started in May 2019 but since we set out on this path together six years ago, her life has changed in ways she never thought possible. Back then she had just quit her job as a museum curator in London so she could find out where her running might take her. A long way as it turned out. The American fitness company Peloton spotted her posting her runs on social media and scooped her up, turning her into one of their star fitness instructors with a big salary to match. 'Now we are both running on air,' I joked when she got the job during the pandemic. 'How funny that both of us are now broadcasting live from studios. It's just you're doing your job on a treadmill and I'm behind a desk.' Her schedule at Peloton's London headquarters is hectic, which means finding a day when we can disappear off to the sea proves almost impossible. So, I strike out alone.

The last 20 miles of the path run along the Hoo Peninsula on the North Kent coast, a thumb-like stretch of land sandwiched between the Thames and the River Medway to the south. The path will take me from Gravesend along the edge of the marshes all the way to the village of Isle of Grain and the North Sea. It is remote out there. There's only one road in and out of the village. I study the Ordnance Survey map intently. For more than 15 miles the footpath runs right along the water. There are no houses or roads for miles. If I get in trouble for any reason, I will be completely on my own.

I set off in June 2025 in a heatwave, on what is forecast to be the hottest day of the year so far. I am counting on a sea breeze to cool me down. I had worked late the night before on the *Ten* and woke at the crack of dawn feeling nervous. 'I'm worried about you going out there alone,' says Richard, who's normally the first to tell me to get out there and do it. 'Can you make sure you've got your phone tracker on so I can see where you are if you get in trouble?' For a moment I think about pulling out, rescheduling it for another cooler day when Susie or one of the others is free to join me. But I want to get this done and I realise I no longer want anyone else to come with me. I have always run with people around me, for company, for support, for safety, for confidence. This is my adventure now and I am going to run it alone.

The train from London St Pancras is a high-speed service that will whisk me out to Gravesend 30 miles away in just over 20 minutes. I step on board early on a Friday morning, going against the flow of commuters, dressed in my running shorts with a backpack full of water, clutching a coffee and a croissant. There'll be nowhere to refill my drinks bottles if I run out and I'm going to need plenty of fluid in this heat.

Gravesend is the final outpost on the path to the sea, the last town on the Thames as I near the end of my 232-mile river journey. I am plunged quickly into the marshlands, low-lying, open, remote. I can see for miles. Just cows and sheep and a lot of birds. The river, almost half a mile wide now, stretches out beside me, flat and calm. Reminders of wars are scattered along the shore: pillboxes, anti-tank obstacles, large forts, now desolate. The Shornemead lighthouse, a red-and-white tube, rises from the water beyond the mudflats, the only vivid colour out here. A huge grey-and-white cargo ship called *Pauline* is heading, like me, towards the North Sea, out past the vast London Gateway container port in Essex on the other side of the river. I see no one. For miles and miles, I run on. It is not easy running. The path is narrow and baked hard in this heat with cracks that are so wide I have to watch where I am putting my feet. *What if I go over on my ankle?* I suddenly think. Help would be hard to find out here and there is nowhere shady to shelter from the sun. *Don't think, just run*, I tell myself. My sense of isolation is compounded by stretches of the path that are so overgrown I have to slow to a walk. I push my way through thigh-high brambles and nettles that scratch and sting my legs and will leave me with itchy welts for several days afterwards.

The Hoo Peninsula is a mysterious, intriguing land, a place apart, lonely, even though it is just 30 miles from London. I am enveloped in its wildness. This land has been mined over the centuries for all that it has: salt, mud, gravel, chalk. Now its old quarries have been flooded and turned into a home for birds, an RSPB nature reserve that is teeming with life. As I run, I see and hear lapwings, skylarks, redshanks, flocks of corn buntings, oystercatchers and sanderlings. From Gravesend to Isle of Grain there is also a surprising amount of death. On the path, fish skeletons, their bones picked clean, and piles and piles of pale white crabs' legs. Nearby their shells lie upside down and empty. The birds have had a fine feast. One, though, wasn't so lucky. A complete set of bird's wings, still attached together, lies in among it all, though the body is missing. The circle of life is strewn for miles beneath my feet.

I stop and watch the vast expanse of slate-grey water. I stop a lot to take it all in. I'm in no hurry. None of my friends are here to chivvy me along, like they normally do. I am well known for liking a 'break' or two when we are out training. No pressure now. This run is about exploring, not pace or time. Around the bend I can see the North Sea now, where the Thames and ocean become one. How strange to think that one day we will scatter our father's ashes into this enormous body of water, our mother's too.

My sister and I had watched Dad being cremated. We hadn't meant to. We didn't know we could. But as we were leaving his funeral, we asked the chapel attendant at the crematorium when his body would go up in flames. 'Your father will be cremated on Monday, in two days' time, at 7 a.m.,' she told us. 'You can come if you want to.' I wasn't going to go. I told Kate that I didn't want to, that I had already said goodbye. But I woke up on that Monday morning at dawn and knew my sister had decided to be with Dad on the very last stretch of his journey. I couldn't let her do it alone. So, as the sun rose, I cycled back along the Thames to the crematorium right on the river, with a flask of freshly made cappuccino in my backpack to share. Dad was famous for making the best coffee. He'd taken it so seriously that he'd even had lessons in latte art until shaky Parkinson's hands put a stop to that too.

His coffin lay on a scissor lift table in a room behind the crematorium's chapel. It was pushed right up against one of the oven doors. The pink and white roses we had picked from his garden on the morning of his funeral lay on top of the coffin where we had left them. They were dead now too. 'Are you ready?', asked the crematorium technician. We nodded. He lifted the metal door, a blast of heat, a deep orange glow and we watched as Dad was shoved into the fire. It was strangely mesmerising. I thought it would be horrifying. I had been afraid to go. Instead, now that I was here, I felt a deep calm. I was glad I was with him. We took turns to look, through a small peephole in the oven door as the flames engulfed his willow coffin. Finally, I knew he had gone; his path had come to an end. We had been with him every step of the way.

For now, his ashes sit in a box in his study back at my parents' house. Grains of bone. I have put them next to a bottle of fine red wine, his beloved camera and the lucky black cat that his father flew with during World War One. I like Dad being back at home. 'Maybe we should keep him here until Mum goes too,' I say to my sister. 'Then they can both float down the Thames together. That's what Mum says she wants to do.'

---

On the Hoo Peninsula, the heat is rising as I head towards the village of Isle of Grain. I am only aware of the temperature when the sea breeze drops and then it is like stepping into an oven. I am wrapped in a sudden humid heat before the wind picks up again and it is gone. It is more than 30°C today, unusually hot for June. I conserve my water and take salt pills, as I did in the Sahara. So many echoes today, so many full circles. I'm glad I'm out here on my own. I can breathe them all in. I've come a long way since that first marathon almost 15 years ago on the streets of London when a lack of water in the heat landed me in a St John Ambulance bay.

Water and air. I didn't have enough of either that day. Since then, I have learnt how to manage myself, to look after my body, to drink enough, to keep moving. Running on air, across sand, through mountains, along rivers. I know now what I need to do to power on. I have played the long game in life, in running, at work. I am still going. I feel strong, stronger than ever before. I think of my father in those last days, starved of water, surviving on nothing but air. And I run on, I push a little harder. Because I can. Because I'm alive. Because he's not.

Two people appear on the sea wall, walking my way. 'You're the first people I have seen out here, and I've been running for 9 miles,' I say, beaming. The woman's eyes widen. 'You're that newsreader,' she says instantly. 'I've just recognised your voice. You know her,' she says to her husband, 'that's Sophie off the news!' They are walking the England Coast Path, they tell me, doing it in chunks. They try to do 300 miles a year if they can. It's a lot but, like me, they love the challenge of ticking off the paths. 'Can we have a selfie?' they ask. 'Take your sunglasses off so we can see you,' says the husband. I do as I'm told, though I wonder just how sweaty and dishevelled I must look right now given they only knew me by my voice.

It is almost 1.30 p.m. when I finally run up the High Street in Isle of Grain. There's only one shop, a Co-op, where I buy water and a juice and a milk smoothie. I'm so thirsty now and hot after almost 20 miles in the sun. It is a straight line, a quarter of a mile left until I hit the sea and the end of my river run. I'm carrying a change of clothes and a small towel, because when I reach that water I am going to jump in, fully clothed. My last steps are along a chalky path across the grass to the sea wall. 'I've made it!' I shout out triumphantly, though there's no one around to hear me. And then I stop in my tracks and laugh out loud. More circles. Just like at the source of the Thames where I started, there is no water here at the finish. It's just vast mudflats that stretch out for what looks like almost a mile. It's low tide. The seawater is so far out that I can't even see the waves breaking. Instead of swimming I just sit. I lower myself slowly down on to the sea wall and let my tired legs dangle over the mud below. I breathe in the air, salty sea air. And then I crack open my bottle of water and I drink and drink and drink.

*Acknowledgements*

I have loved writing this book. My editor at Bloomsbury, Charlotte Croft, first suggested the idea in 2018 when we were introduced at the Cheltenham Literature festival a few months after the Marathon des Sables. I said yes, maybe, I'll think about it, let's chat. And then stalled for about 5 years. I wasn't sure if I could write a book. I wasn't sure what I would write. But Charlotte (like my husband) does not let me give up and she nudged and nudged me year after year until I finally plucked up the courage to start writing it all down. I am so glad she did. Thank you to Charlotte, Caroline Hewlett, Rachel Nicholson, all the team at Bloomsbury, Lizzie Davies for the audiobook and my literary agent, Julian Alexander, for getting me over the line.

When I finally did start writing, the first person I tested it all out on was Brian Hollywood, a very talented BBC producer, friend and a beautiful writer. I owe him huge thanks for always finding the time and for always coming back with such good observations and thoughts. He gave me the confidence to keep going.

Andy Dixon and Rick Pearson at *Runner's World* magazine asked me to start writing a monthly column for them in 2023. It has proved an invaluable way to think about running in all its guises. Thank you both for getting me on board. I really enjoy working with you.

I have been 'on air' for a lot longer than I have been running. I love my job at the BBC, and I love working with the teams of editors, producers, directors and correspondents in the newsroom at Broadcasting House. Thanks to all of you past and present, not just for making work so interesting and challenging and fun, but also for just about tolerating my running chat over the years.

My sister Kate Raworth came up with the title for this book long before I had written a single word. She and her teenage twins Cas and Siri were also my first 'readers'. They printed off the manuscript and then sat in a line on holiday in Croatia passing page after page to each other as they all read it. Thank you for such great comments, for finding typos, for asking pertinent questions and making spot on suggestions along the way.

The photo on the front of this book was taken by my father as I was about to cross the finish line at the 2016 London Marathon. I was running to raise money for Cure Parkinson's that year. Dad had just been diagnosed with the disease. I am so sad that he isn't here to see his photograph on the front of my book. He would have been so proud.

I read this book to my parents as I was writing it, knowing that Dad probably wouldn't be here by the time it was published. I wrote a lot of the last chapter sitting next to him as he died and read it aloud to him anyway. I hope he heard it. Thank you to my mother, Jenny, for always cheering me on throughout life. You and Dad have been the most wonderful, generous parents, always encouraging us to give everything a go.

## ACKNOWLEDGEMENTS

Since my first marathon I have almost always had an online coach telling me what to do every week, someone to answer to. Karen Weir, Liz Yelling, David Chalfen and Jo Wilkinson, thank you all for your expert guidance, encouragement and support over the years. I never imagined I would get faster and faster in my 40s and 50s but that's what you helped me do. Sir Brendan Foster changed my life with his Great North Run. Then Hugh Brasher and Penny Dain at the London Marathon took it to another level. Thanks to all of them for the inspiration and support over the years, and to Professor John Brewer for giving me the confidence to give marathon running another go after my first attempt. He ran with me on the day to stop me being scared of collapsing.

I assumed long distance running was a lonely sport. How wrong I was. I have made some of my best friends in races, on footpaths, in the desert and the mountains. From the Cavalcade, Tent 128 and the desert gang to the Six Star crew, the Kew Runners and my ever-growing parkrun pack. There are too many of you to name but you know who you are. All of you have helped, cajoled, inspired, pushed and dragged me over thousands of miles since I began running 20 years ago. Thank you for all the friendship, laughter, tears, inspiration, injury angsting, advice, snacks, support and chat. I feel so lucky to have found you all.

To Mimi, who resigned and unresigned a few times over the years. You have been spectacular. Thank you always for being there for the kids and for us.

Ella, Georgie and Ollie, you three are hands down the best and most wonderful achievements of my life. I couldn't be prouder of you all. I wrote this for you.

And last but very definitely not least, to my husband, Richard, who was the first to inspire me to run long distances and is still the first to tell me to get on with it when I'm wavering, the first to tell me I can do it when I think I can't. Thank you for so many years of love, support, kindness and constant encouragement. I wouldn't have done it without you.